GREENHOUSE GARDENING

GREENHOUSE GARDENING

Ian Walls

WARD LOCK LIMITED LONDON

ISBN 0 7063 1126 4

Ward Lock Limited,
116 Baker Street,
London W1M 2BB

PRINTED IN SPAIN

Contents

INTRODUCTION

A temperate climate, while admirable for many aspects of gardening, imposes considerable restrictions on the range of crops which can be grown out of doors with regularity and precision. Matters are still further complicated by the tremendously wide variance in temperature, exposure, rainfall, and sunshine possible within the boundaries of what is, relatively speaking, a small country.

Perhaps this is why more and more gardeners are becoming interested in the cultivation of crops and plants in greenhouses, where the climate can, to a very large extent in this modern day and age, be dictated by the turn of a switch, and gardening can become a twelve month hobby instead of the brief sojourn it often is when relying entirely on outside culture. Thanks also to modern structural materials and improved methods of glass retention, greenhouses need not now be the subject of constant maintenance they once were. Automatic controls for heating, ventilation, humidity and watering will constantly keep a watchful eye on things, and at a reasonable cost too. It can be seen, therefore, that greenhouse gardening can now be a most painless form of gardening. The amenity value of a greenhouse is something which not everyone really appreciates until the results are forthcoming in the form of year-round colour and interest, succulent fresh fruit and vegetables out of season, and the ability to raise young plants for eventual garden culture.

It would be wrong to imagine that everyone can immediately become an expert at growing crops or plants in a greenhouse, as, while the basic rules of gardening apply, there are subtle differences between popping something into the open garden on a long-term basis, and producing a plant from a seed or cutting in a heated greenhouse in a matter of a few weeks. Yet the rudimentary instincts of gardening are something which are, I feel, inherent in most of us, whether we have been brought up in town or country, and it is merely a question of asking ourselves precisely what we want to achieve in the whole realm of growing things. If there is any aspiration in the direction of a greenhouse, whether heated or cold, then the challenge is there to take up, and I feel sure it will open up completely new horizons for gardeners.

I will endeavour, in the pages which follow, to deal at a thoroughly practical and realistic level with as many of the facets of greenhouse gardening as space allows. I will also bear in mind at all times that there are many ways of achieving excellent results, and will therefore merely try to set down the general rules, emphasising what I feel are the really vital issues according to the experience I have so far gained over a lifetime of gardening in many different spheres in this and other countries.

Ian G. Walls

1 General factors

Before embarking on the cultivation of anything, I feel it is essential to put things into the right perspective, speaking largely from the meteorological standpoint at this stage.

Differing climates are caused largely by latitudinal placement, a southern area usually enjoying higher average temperatures because it is nearer the equator. The tremendous influence of the Gulf Stream can, however, result in unique warm pockets in both north and south, this having particular significance for the whole of the western sea board. In general the coastal areas have more equable temperatures due to the thermal warmth from the immense bulk of the sea, but they can also be extremely exposed, and this has special significance in the realm of greenhouse culture, as we shall see later when discussing heat loss. The same is true of exposed areas anywhere, often necessitating the planning of effective shelter.

Both total sunshine figures and total radiation, the latter taking into account total light intensity as distinct from bright sunshine, have profound effects on the rate of growth of any green plant which depends on light for the vital process of photosynthesis, and this is a very important facet of greenhouse culture. On this theme one must take into account the reduction of light occasioned by smoke pollution, both physically restricting the passage of light or staining the glass or plastic of a greenhouse in industrial areas. Obviously coastal and country areas, untroubled by atmospheric pollution, have a big advantage, and a still further bonus of a coastal area is the reflected light from the sea, which can be very considerable.

Rainfall figures, while greatly affecting the growth of outside crops, cannot be said to have a great bearing on the growth of plants protected by a greenhouse, it being obvious, of course, that when it is raining it is generally cloudy and the light intensity is therefore lower, and there is, of course, a general rise in humidity. I do feel, however, that consideration of these variable factors by the enthusiastic gardener is frequently overlooked – to such an extent that disappointment is sometimes inevitable. It takes but a little time to check up on the situation regarding sunshine figures, average temperature, exposure, rainfall, and atmospheric pollution, by consulting meteorological records in your local library. The weather or its associated factors cannot be changed at will and must, of course, be accepted in any particular area. Yet assessing things intelligently will condition the mind to what results can reasonably be expected in any district.

LIGHT INTENSITIES
In terms of the amateur greenhouse, one must therefore expect growth rate to be pro-rata with the light received at different times of the year, which means that it may be very difficult, if not impossible, for the gardener with a greenhouse in a northern area to grow as early and heavy a crop of light-demanding tomatoes as his counterpart in a southern area without artificial light to balance the deficit. But this need not deter the enthusiast one little bit when one remembers that not all crops are so greedy for light, nor are most gardeners impressed with the need for early and maximum crops. One can also instance many pot plants and propagation activities where intense light is extremely undesirable, to say the least.

Exposure to wind is a matter which certainly must be taken well into account, particularly with constantly rising heating costs. Gardeners are frequently warned about avoiding 'frost pockets' in regard to greenhouse placement, and while a low-lying area into which cold air drains may indeed make greater temporary demands on any heating system, the air in a 'frost pocket' is normally more 'still' due to the sheltered nature of the area, which can often nullify any additional heating costs on a long-term basis.

The crux of the matter is whether or not any particular site is worth considering for the erection of a greenhouse. I would think, however, that there are few gardens which cannot accommodate a greenhouse of one sort of another, but it is important to choose the best type of greenhouse for that particular site, and at the same time take into account where one's interests lie, as I feel there must be some reconciliation between these two basic factors. It would, for example, be pointless for a gardener in the city garden where atmospheric pollution is a problem and where there is also considerable sun shut-off caused by buildings, to think in terms of putting up a greenhouse especially for the purpose of growing light-demanding crops such as *early* tomatoes. It would be much more rational, in this case, to consider the mildly heated greenhouse for certain aspects of propagation, pot plants, and perhaps a few later tomatoes and chrysanthemums in pots.

The position is entirely different for the gardener with a sunny and not excessively exposed garden in an area free from all atmospheric pollution. Here a greenhouse with an efficient heating system can be used for salads, followed by an early crop of tomatoes, all of which are light demanding. Chrysanthemums, of course, can then be grown in the autumn, and pot plants through the winter.

One's thoughts too may often be not so much on a greenhouse as a separate entity, but on a greenhouse as a conservatory or glass porch for various activities, particularly pot plant growing.

The slope or otherwise of any garden may well have some bearing on the erection of a greenhouse, particularly where a very sloping site is involved. A still further matter, frequently overlooked, is the state of the soil in the proposed erection area, this being of paramount importance when crops such as tomatoes or salad crops are to be grown in the greenhouse borders. Drainage too is important, although this can be attended to fairly simply in most cases (see page 15). The incidence of pests, diseases, and weeds must also be fully taken into account. There can be many a disappointment when the presence of potato root eelworm, with its devastating effect on tomatoes, is overlooked, necessitating alter-

11

native growing methods to border culture or initial soil sterilisation. This is easily checked up on by contacting your local advisory service regarding an eelworm count, it being advisable to ask at the same time for a general soil analysis. Weeds too can be a problem, especially deep rooting types such as horsetail, coltsfoot, convolvulus and many more, and while it may seem simple enough to control the weeds in the limited area of a greenhouse, the presence of obnoxious weeds in the general outside area will mean a constant invasion of the weeds into the greenhouse, demanding a general weed control programme for the whole area.

The range of permutations along these lines is endless, the final decision being a happy marriage between available and carefully assessed conditions and the sensible utilisation of the greenhouse, conservatory or porch eventually erected.

WHAT TYPE OF GREENHOUSE SHOULD I BUILD?
If one visits an old estate garden or some of the older established Botanic Gardens or public parks, the type of greenhouse in evidence is invariably a stoutly constructed massive wooden structure with thick metal internal members. Many of these greenhouses are built against a south wall for maximum catchment of the sun and also to ensure maximum stability. It is of interest that the wall was invariably painted white to reflect light, one issue often overlooked by modern designers. Older type greenhouses not built against a wall are also sure to be stoutly constructed on a thick base wall. Many of these greenhouses are now a considerable age and yet are still in good repair, which is surely mute testimony to their quality, both with regard to general design and the materials with which they were built. Nevertheless, unless the wood was teak or oak, you can be sure that these greenhouses have been painted dozens of times during their lifetime, and have possibly been reglazed with new putty a few times, for good measure.

It would be very costly these days to emulate the structural esigns of these early greenhouses, and not particularly desirable in many ways, even if initial cost was no deterrent. These older structures seldom blend with modern architecture. They also have such a large opaque material to glass ratio that a considerable amount of natural light is excluded and they pose a constant maintenance problem, even if superior timber is used. Finally, the inadequacy of ventilation, in some cases, and the narrowness of doors, show that old-fashioned greenhouses have little part to play in modern gardening.

One redeeming feature of these early greenhouses is the way in which they both store up sun heat and retain artificial heat, because of their excellent draught-free construction, and this gives a vital clue to the selection of a modern greenhouse. Choose as sturdily and well built a type as is currently available, compatible with large pane size of glass, build it on a good base wall, and you will have a greenhouse which, although not completely ideal for light transmission, retains heat. Such a structure is suitable for year-round use for pot plants, propagation and other purposes where heat is important. If an all-glass greenhouse is selected with no base wall at all (other than the foundations) maximum light will certainly be transmitted, which is particularly desirable for salad crops, tomatoes and the like. During the winter months, however, it will be found that it is much more costly to heat such a greenhouse. If running costs are not important, however, there is no doubt that the all-glass structure is better for all purposes because of its light transmission virtues.

Specific types of greenhouses will shortly be discussed, and all that is necessary at this stage is to realise that greenhouses are of different designs and forms and that their purpose must necessarily vary accordingly, largely on the grounds of culture and economics.

PROVISION OF SERVICES
A most important facet of greenhouse utilisation is the provision of services, this referring to adequate supplies of water and electricity, and, to a lesser extent, drainage of rain water.

WATER SUPPLY
A good supply of water for all greenhouse activities is essential, and precisely how this can be achieved will depend a great deal on the general water situation. A permanent supply

of water led from the household system will require the permission of the appropriate Water Board, as few local authorities will allow a permanent take-off from the main unless they give formal permission. Some authorities may insist on the water being separately metered and invoice the water accordingly at an agreed rate of payment. Provided permission is given for a permanent pipe, this must be led to the greenhouse at a suitable depth underground, to avoid freezing. Preferably this is a job for a plumber, at least as far as connection to the main is concerned, although it is quite a simple matter to lay alkathene pipes. The diameter of the supply pipe is again a matter for Water Board approval. Where hose and can watering is largely to be the rule, a small diameter supply pipe may be adequate, but when spraylines or mist propagation units are to be used, these demand a good volume and pressure of water, around 40–60 lbs. per sq. in., and one will require to think in terms of a 1-in. supply pipe at least. Alternatively a 'near permanent' supply in the form of an underground alkathene or steel pipeline can have a temporary connection to an outside tap, such as one already in existence in a garage, and few Water Boards object to this procedure. A problem with this sort of arrangement is that water may be left in the pipe during cold weather, and this can result in damage.

The many problems of an adequate water supply are sometimes difficult to overcome in certain districts, and commercial growers frequently install corrugated steel butyl lined tanks, the outlet being controlled with an electric pump, which is the same principle involved on a much smaller scale for mist irrigation units (see Chapter 9).

ELECTRICITY SUPPLY
While it is relatively simple to install a supply of electricity in a greenhouse, either by overhead lines or underground cables, I feel this is a task best left entirely to a qualified electrician. Often, however, preliminary work can be carried out, leaving the connecting up to the main supply to the electrician. It is necessary to ensure adequate loading for all the electrical equipment likely to be used in the greenhouse in the forseeable future. 100 watts for light, + $2\frac{1}{2}$ Kw for heaters,

with odd items such as soil warming for a bench or a mist irrigation unit in addition to this, can add up to a total loading of 4 or 5 Kw, and this loading involves the use of a fairly heavy cable and a connecting right back to the meter, definitely work for the *qualified* person.

DRAINAGE

Something frequently overlooked is the provision of drains to take away water shed by the roof of the greenhouse, which can be considerable if the greenhouse is large. In the case of small greenhouses, gutters are frequently not provided and drainage is necessary in the land adjacent to the greenhouse. In this case tile or rubble drains should be run along the area of reception and linked to a convenient field drain outlet, or alternatively a seep hole. Where there are gutters and down pipes, these should preferably be linked to a convenient drain, although again a seep hole can be provided. A barrel can also be used for limited amounts of catchment.

PLANNING PERMISSION FOR GREENHOUSE ERECTION

Planning regulations vary from area to area, but in general a small greenhouse (or shed) round about 6 × 8 ft. can be erected in many places without planning permission. This, however, will require local confirmation. Greenhouses above a certain size are usually the subject of planning permission, either by local or county committees, according to the size and nature of the greenhouse in question. Normally it is a case of providing 1, a location plan of the proposed erection – a general plan of the area can often be obtained by applying to your local authority and paying a small fee, it then merely being a question of drawing in the location of the greenhouse in red ink, preferably to the correct scale; 2, details of the greenhouse and its foundations. Ideally this should consist of side and end elevations with dimensions and notes on the dimensions of the main structural members. All this information is readily available from greenhouse manufacturers, whereas if you are building your own greenhouse it will be necessary to draw up a set of plans, or have these made up for you. Notes should also be given on any drainage plans if these involve linkage to ducted drains;

3, it is usually necessary to obtain permission in writing from your landlord and also perhaps two or three of your neighbours, and this is sent in to support your application for planning permission; 4, any special requirements or adherence to building lines will be clearly stated by the appropriate authority and it is as well to find out something about these *before* going into things too deeply and ordering a specific type of greenhouse.

The position regarding these matters appears to vary in different parts of the country and I would emphasise that one should enquire precisely what is demanded by the appropriate authority at the outset.

2 The importance of greenhouse design

I have indicated earlier that the modern gardener is becoming much more discriminating over the choice of a greenhouse, and quite rightly so. Commercial growers have come through a period of intense sophistication in greenhouse design, and will now only accept a structure which reaches a very high standard on many counts. The main features of a modern greenhouse can be summarised under the following headings.

QUICK EASY ERECTION
Greenhouses are now invariably prefabricated in the factory. Ease of erection varies according to the type of house, and one should always take care to find out precisely at what stage of prefabrication the house is delivered and that erection plans from the manufacturer are completely detailed and accurate.

The greenhouse shown here is of metal
and glass on a base of brickwork
and is virtually maintenance free

African violets require at least
twelve hours of light during
the day; seed in Spring

COMPLETELY MAINTENANCE-FREE AFTER ERECTION

By virtue of the structural components being either pressure treated soft woods, aluminium alloy, galvanised or enamelled steel, maintenance is virtually nil after erection. Glazing methods should avoid entirely the use of putty, which tends to harden and flake in a few years. This involves either dry glazing (the glass sliding into grooves), clip glazing on a seal of plastic beading, non-hardening bitumen, or other patent method. Putty glazed houses are becoming less popular annually, and rightly so. Freedom from maintenance varies enormously according to house type and design, and the following will give guidance on the main range of materials:

MAIN STRUCTURAL MATERIALS
USED IN GREENHOUSES

Material	Strength/Bulk Ratio	Cost	Durability
Redwood	Medium	Low	Good if painted or treated
Red Cedar	Low	Medium	Good
Imported hardwood	Medium	High	Good
Burma teak	High	High	Very good
Oak	High	High	Good
Steel	Very high	Low	Rusts unless galvanised or painted regularly
Cast iron	Medium/high	Medium	Less liable to rust
Reinforced concrete	Low	Medium	Good
Aluminium alloy	High	Medium	Believed good
Pressure-treated softwoods	Variable	Low	Good

LIGHT TRANSMISSION

This should be optimal by virtue of the ratio of glass to opaque material being high and the avoidance of heavy light restricting structural members. The importance of light for the general growth of plants will be referred to in many instances throughout this book. At this stage it will perhaps suffice to say that light is the life blood of plants which manufacture carbohydrates in their leaves during the day and use this up during the night. It is therefore important to balance day and night temperatures accordingly, to avoid a surplus or deficit of carbohydrate.

In the earlier days of greenhouses referred to in the previous chapter, it was common to find a pane width of 12–14 in., whereas nowadays it is frequently as wide as $28\frac{3}{4}$ in. (Dutch light size).

A further important consideration is the shape of the greenhouse. The angle of the incidence of the sun varies considerably between winter and summer (Fig. 1). The further north one travels, the more acute the angle of incidence, although in the north the days are longer during summer because of the bigger arc of the sun, and shorter in winter due to the shorter arc. The effect this has on effective light transmission in a greenhouse is profound, as the nearer normal (90°) the angle of incidence of sunlight to glass, the greater the absorption, glass being able to transmit slightly more than 90% of the total outside light and solar short wave heat. The conventional sloping roof of a span roofed greenhouse (see p. 23) with its length orientated east west deflects most of the sunlight from the roof during winter, absorbing most of it through the vertical side wall. Once the sun rises higher on the horizon, the roof will also absorb direct radiation, but still largely on the south facing slope. This means that dense crop growth on the south side will shade the crop at the rear of the house, although the sun's rays will readily penetrate the back of the house otherwise. A bench along the south facing side of the greenhouse is of course the ideal place for winter propagation or for the growing of any crop which demands all available light, such as young tomatoes or certain types of pot plants, provided the vertical side wall is high enough.

Turn the same greenhouse with the ridge running north south and the situation alters, only the south facing gable end being favourably placed for winter light, whereas in the summer months there is an equable distribution of light to both roofs of the greenhouse. On balance therefore the east/west orientation is perhaps more valuable to the average gardener, especially where there are winter activities.

Considerable experimentation has taken place over many years on the best shape of greenhouse for maximum light absorption, the best known of which was carried out by the John Innes Horticultural Institution when at Bayford-bury many years ago. Broadly speaking these experiments involved the presentation of a better configuration to absorb the winter sun.

Curvilinear houses of east/west orientation have a fairly large section of glass favourably placed for sun admission at virtually any time of the year, because of their semi-rounded nature, and indeed there is much to be said for them on this score. Greenhouses aiming at the same basic principles are now being designed with curved roofs, or may be of a completely circular design, one type of which can be rotated to catch maximum sun. It is of interest to note that the use of curved roofs is by no means a new conception, either for immense Botanic Garden type structures or for those of amateur size.

The quality of glass used for greenhouses is important. Normally 24 oz. horticultural glass is the rule, and this should be smooth and unwarped to permit even distribution of light. Continental grades of glass are slightly heavier (26 oz.), and the larger Dutch light size used for some types of structures is 32 oz. It is of interest to note that in very sunny countries clear glass is not used for greenhouses, translucent types being preferred.

STABILITY
Despite the need for good light transmission, a greenhouse must be completely stable in design and able to withstand really strong winds. The important issue in the avoidance of wind damage is the reduction of astragal vibration resulting in broken panes of glass. Exposed sites are particularly vulnerable and shelter may be necessary, provided this does not restrict the light (see Chapter 4). Stable characteristics of any greenhouse depend entirely on overall design, and one would feel that any established supplier of repute would make very certain that all stress factors were carefully calculated.

VENTILATION

This should be adequate, the now accepted norm being a ventilation ratio of at least one fifth of the floor area. It must be emphasised that this calculation applies only when vents are capable of being opened really adequately. It is a fact that many small amateur-type glasshouses have a very poor ventilation ratio. Note that where extractor fan ventilation or pressurised air conditioning is selected in lieu of conventional ventilators, the air change rate should be in the order of 50 to 60 per hour, and information on this point is available from the supplier of the fans and ancillary equipment. The modern thinking along the lines of 'air conditioning' greenhouses with fully automated controls for ventilation, humidity, heat control etc., along with CO_2 enrichment has much to commend it, and these are matters which will be discussed in more detail in Chapter 7. There can be no doubt that a more precise control of greenhouse environment is certainly needed, and while commercial growers have been quick to grasp this because their livelihood depends on it, amateur gardeners are still rather reluctant to think in terms of automatic controls. This subject will be discussed further in Chapter 8.

FREEDOM OF MOVEMENT

The door and general design of a greenhouse should be such that it allows freedom of movement, easy entry of barrows, adequate head room and so on. Doors should open inwards, or be of the sliding type. Perhaps this is not so vital for the amateur gardener as for the commercial grower, but it should still be regarded as an issue of some importance.

INITIAL COST

This should be reasonable and at a level compatible with features provided. The initial cost of a greenhouse is something which can readily be ascertained from various manufacturers.

3. Types of greenhouses

While, in a sense, any type of greenhouse can be used for any cultural activity provided the necessary heat level can be maintained, it is common sense to select the type of greenhouse best suited to the intended purpose. The advantages of a good marriage between design and purpose largely lie in cultural benefits and reduced heating costs. Possibly the best place to see all greenhouse types side by side is at one of the larger flower shows or a modern garden centre, but it is nevertheless a good idea to be well informed before you look or buy.

CULTURAL ASPECTS IN RELATION TO GREENHOUSE TYPE

Reference has been made earlier to the need of some crops for maximum light, and this will apply to all salad crops grown in the border or on the ground of the greenhouse, tomatoes and cucumbers, especially in their early stages, and also flower crops such as chrysanthemums grown by the direct planted method. Houses with base walls are more suited to benched crops and propagation, although they will suffice admirably for a more advanced crop grown from ground level, this applying particularly to traditionally grown pot chrysanthemums of the mid and late flowering varieties.

HEATING COSTS IN RELATION TO GREENHOUSE TYPE

The greater the ratio of glass to opaque material, and in particular when there are no base walls of brick or composition block, the greater is the heat loss sustained by the greenhouse during periods when there is little direct solar radiation, which will be on most cool dull days, and during the night. On average it will generally be more costly to retain an 'all-glass' type of greenhouse at the requisite temperature than it will be to maintain a base wall type at the same temperature.

Having said all this, one must now move on to the stage where a decision has to be made concerning what actual temperature the greenhouse is to be maintained at. The answer is a useful and additional guide to the selection of greenhouse type, it being important not to confuse the three quite separate issues of type, purpose and level of heating.

STOVE OR HOT CONDITIONS – For orchids, high temperature propagation, tender plants, palms, etc – never below 65°F.

INTERMEDIATE OR WARM CONDITIONS – Maintained at a temperature never below 55°F. – plants including tomatoes, cucumber and the like, for full-season use, winter and summer, for pot plants and varied propagation.

COOL CONDITIONS – The term 'cool' refers to completely unheated conditions in summer, artificial heat only being used during the autumn/winter/spring months, when frost protection and little else is the aim, the temperature being maintained at around 45°F. Such a temperature is ideal for the average gardener wishing only to over-winter non-hardy plants, dahlia tubers and other stock, and carry out a reasonable range of not-too-early propagation activities in the spring, followed by crops such as tomatoes during the summer. The economics of this range of activities are most likely to fit in to the pattern deemed necessary by many gardeners.

COLD CONDITIONS – Here no artificial heat at all is provided, all heat being derived from solar heat input, which limits the house to spring/summer/autumn use, although much will depend on the specific district involved. The value of a cold greenhouse culturally can be much greater in a mild southern area than in a cold northern one where, if conditions are exposed, there may be difficulty in growing worthwhile crops of many things. It should be emphasised that the completely unheated greenhouse is more or less *useless* for over-wintering non-hardy plants of any type, unless the winter should prove an abnormally mild one and the greenhouse is sited in an area where frost is seldom experienced, a situation which is extremely uncommon in Britain. It could also be said that if conditions are so favourable out of doors, then the need for a greenhouse diminishes.

SPECIFIC GREENHOUSE TYPES
Span-roofed houses

Greenhouses are largely classified according to the design of the roof. Span-roofed houses have either perpendicular or slightly sloping sides with a pitched roof rising to a ridge in the centre, the angle of which can vary considerably, especially with modern designs. Greenhouses with lapped glass tend to have a steeper pitch than those of unlapped Dutch design. It is unwise to have too flat a roof pitch in districts where heavy snow is probable, to avoid snow load damage, especially where the house is unheated.

There can be base walls of brick or composition block of various heights, generally around 2–3 ft., on which the greenhouse structure is built, or these can be weatherboard, metal, asbestos or plastic base 'walls'. Alternatively there may be no base wall other than the foundations, the glass extending to ground level. Gutter or eaves height is generally between 4 ft. 6 in. and 6 ft., and ridge height is according to width, generally around 2–3 feet higher than gutters or eaves. A brick, composition block, wood or even asbestos base wall reduces the glass area but increases the insulation properties, rendering the greenhouse, as already stated, a more economic proposition for year-round use in respect of heating costs, and a most useful structure for specialised pot plant culture or propagation. Some types of houses have a base 'wall' at one side and are glazed to ground level at the other, preferably the south side, an ideal compromise in many instances. Span roofed houses are available in a range of materials, the qualities of which have been previously referred to (see page 17). While all types are normally provided in prefabricated form, there is nothing to prevent the do-it-yourself enthusiast from building a greenhouse of any suitable size and design, provided the consideration is taken of the long-term maintenance issues. Ventilators are situated in the roof and also, in some cases, on the sides, unless extractor fans are fitted, in which case ventilators may be reduced merely to provide an adequate air inlet (see page 51). Size of greenhouse can vary from 6 × 4ft. to any desired module, a very useful type of house being around 12 × 8 ft. as this allows for 3 ft. benches and a 2 ft. path, or two practical sized growing borders.

Lean-to houses

While, for a period, lean-to houses were distinctly unpopular due to ventilation and directional light problems, coupled with 'overheating' in summer, they are again now much in vogue, principally because it is often convenient and more economical to extend domestic heating systems into the greenhouse. This is particularly so when the greenhouse is constructed on the wall of the dwelling house. Ventilation can now be readily effected by fan systems and one-sided light is not a vital issue with many activities. Lean-to greenhouses can have either a single pitch or three-quarter pitch roof, the latter only being of real advantage where the ridge of the greenhouse can be extended above the top level of the rear wall, thus allowing conventional ventilators to be fitted on both sides of the ridge. In both cases, side or front ventilators can also be fitted to give a through current of air, although extractor fans obviate the need for this. Lean-to greenhouses are best sited due south, although some slight variation of orientation is not vital, and indeed where the greenhouse is also used as a conservatory, west facing orientation has many advantages for the evening sun. North facing houses are of course useful for ferns, certain alpines, and shade loving pot plants. The constructional detail of lean-to greenhouses can follow the same varied pattern as span roofed houses.

Porches

Porches often come into the same category as lean-to houses and can be exceedingly useful for a wide range of plants and activities, in addition to domestic uses, but draughts and constant chilling can be a problem in winter, due to frequent opening and shutting of doors.

Dutch light houses

As distinct from glass to ground level houses, some of which are often termed 'Dutch type', the true Dutch light greenhouse consists of Dutch light frame sashes, each measuring approximately 5 ft. × 2½ ft. with tongued and grooved side rails bracketed together to form an extremely stable greenhouse. These houses are very popular with growers of lettuce, tomatoes, chrysanthemums etc., but less popular for propagation and pot plant work, principally because they are glass to ground level and also because their grooved glazing system allows a certain degree of heat loss, as it is essential for the glass to be held fairly loosely to avoid wind damage. They are, however, inexpensive to buy and extremely simple to erect, this therefore making them popular. The size of a single span Dutch light greenhouse is in the order of 12–13 ft. wide, although the sloping sides and low overall height restrict head and working room, unless the whole house is built up on a brick base wall. Multi-span blocks of Dutch light houses are also popular, although in recent years the Venlo type, 10 ft. 6 in. wide (3 metres) of Continental design, has tended to oust the Dutch light structure. Both these types are, however, only likely to interest the commercial grower.

Dutch light greenhouses can readily be modified so that they are mobile, with pulley wheels and base blocks fitted with an angle iron as rails. The gable ends of the house are hinged, to lift off or up in order to clear a standing crop. The basic principle is to practise a crop rotation system under glass, and this is readily achieved over three or more plots where the site is flat. A simple rotation could involve a crop of lettuce covered until March or early April, the house then being pushed on to the second position to give a crop of tomatoes, and finally, in late September/October on to cover a crop of chrysanthemums which had been planted in May. The following year the crops are changed around to give each a new site, although there are obviously a great many possible permutations. The extra cost involved in a mobile greenhouse is around 25% to 30%, and this, coupled with the room they take up and the probems of heating, together with the effectiveness of modern chemical soil sterilisation, has tended to make them less popular than they were a few years ago.

Curvilinear or Mansard houses

These have been referred to earlier (see page 19). They have excellent light transmission properties and make ideal general purpose greenhouses, especially for propagation and pot plant work. Popular types are constructed of alloy or treated steel and are extremely sturdy. They can be obtained in different sizes and in lean-to form.

Circular houses

These have only recently become available, but obviously round type greenhouses will grow in popularity as their light transmission virtues become more widely appreciated, especially as they can be turned to catch the sun. Ventilators should preferably be of the extractor fan type, or should have an air conditioning system installed, otherwise excessive sun heat build-up is likely to be a problem in the summer due to their excellent solar heat transmission.

Plastic greenhouses

The use of 500 or 1,000 gauge polythene or P.V.C., along with various other reinforced plastic materials for the construction of greenhouses, is not new. Yet in more recent years the design of plastic greenhouses has improved to such an extent that the excessive ultra-violet breakdown and mechanical stress of the plastic materials has been considerably reduced. There are several ways of securing the plastic, each of which has its own virtues and failings. European types are designed on rather different principles. There are numerous designs of plastic houses, some of which can be built on the do-it-yourself basis, while others can be bought complete. While the do-it-yourself types tend to be rather flimsy, the more sophisticated forms are extremely stable. The 'Bubble' house has attracted attention in recent years, the plastic being kept inflated by a fan, and ventilation is effected by an ancillary fan which operates a counterbalanced ventilator. In the most general of terms, the thinner grades of polythene must be considered as having a very limited life – perhaps two years at most, although a longer life is claimed for P.V.C. Damage by wind is most likely following a period of bright light, the plastic having been weakened by the ultra-violet rays although U.V.-proofed forms are now available. Plastics also tend to become cloudy and dirty, as dust readily clings because of static electrical adhesion. The light transmission ability of plastic greenhouses is excellent due to the light structural members and also because *all* the light in a plastic house is diffused and not direct. Polythene, unlike glass, does not trap the long heat waves transmitted back by soil and fitments, and P.V.C., although similar in this respect, is slightly less so. This means in practical terms that sun heat is readily lost when solar radiation ceases.

The low initial cost of the do-it-yourself plastic greenhouse, and the simplicity with which it can be built and, in time, the plastic replaced, makes it an attractive proposition. Fan ventilation is, however, more or less a necessity in order to reduce condensation, and this of course adds to the initial cost. Whether or not the more sophisticated and therefore more expensive forms of plastic greenhouses are worthy of consideration will depend much on personal preference and, perhaps more than anything, on the ability to erect and move the greenhouse around easily to permit crop rotation, thus avoiding the need for soil sterilisation. Really firm anchorage to the ground is necessary with all types, and the more flimsy forms would require additional support for a 'strung up' crop such as tomatoes or cucumber.

SUMMARY OF TYPES AND ACTIVITIES

GREENHOUSE TYPE	SPECIAL FEATURES	RANGE OF ACTIVITIES
SPAN-ROOFED (wood, alloy, steel, concrete)	Brick base wall	Pot plants, propagation, chrysanths in pots.
	Weatherboard base wall	Not so advantageous in respect of heat retention, but base "wall" can be lined with insulating materials such as fibre glass.
	Glass to ground level	More costly to heat, but better light transmission makes them ideal for ground grown crops.
LEAN-TO (Single pitch or ¾-span)	With or without base wall	Will grow most crops, but there can be problems with ventilation and overheating unless extractor fans are installed. Light distribution unequal. Excellent for peaches etc. against wall.
DUTCH LIGHT	Static	Ideal for summer crops. Frequently used for lettuce and tomatoes. Heat loss occasioned by loose glazing system.
	Mobile	Allows a system of crop rotation which can be highly advantageous.
CULVILINEAR	On small base wall	Ideal for most activities, as in the case of glass to ground level types. Heat loss fairly high with the latter.
CIRCULAR	Still in fairly early stages of development	Particularly good for pot plant culture and propagation. Fan ventilation or 'air conditioning' is likely to be beneficial.
PLASTIC	'Do-it-yourself' type	Will grow most crops with equal dexterity, provided crop support is adequate. Fan ventilation essential.
	Sophisticated type	Excellent for all activities, with added advantages of mobility. Fan ventilation is still essential.

4 Site selection and erection procedures

There has been sufficient discussion in Chapter 1 regarding light transmission and exposure for these matters to be given the consideration they deserve when a greenhouse is to be built. The convenience of any particular position for a greenhouse should not be allowed to over-rule the importance of good sun reception for as long a daily period as possible, both summer and winter, and it is a fairly simple matter to observe this carefully over a period, noting the shade occasioned by trees or buildings and remembering that the sun is high in June but low in December.

Shelter too must be considered, to avoid damage and excessive heat loss, it often being necessary to accept some compromise between shelter and loss of sun for a short daily period. In very exposed areas the placement of a greenhouse between due north/south hedges or other forms of shelter is best, as this allows open exposure to the south. There will be some loss of sun morning and evening (Fig. 3), but strong due south/west winds are overcome. Try to keep the greenhouse at least 10–15 ft. from a hedge or shelter media, to avoid both undue shade and, in the case of trees, root growth. With tree belts a greater distance should be allowed. Deciduous hedges or tree belts have, of course, the advantage of allowing some penetration of winter sun when bereft of leaves. With all forms of shelter it is better to filter wind rather than stop it abruptly, a practice which causes turbulence. This is why open type fences, 'permeable' brick walls, plastic mesh, and all natural media, are often much more preferable than solid type walls or fences, although privacy must also be considered in many cases for exposed areas.

SOME TYPES OF SHELTER MEDIA
Artificial (which should be at least 6 ft. tall)

a) Plastic mesh, close mesh wire netting or hessian screens, erected on stout supports.
b) Interwoven or lap fencing, preferable to open type where privacy has to be considered.
c) Various types of wooden fencing, provided these are about 50% permeable (again privacy having a bearing on things).
d) Brick or composition block walls, permeable bricks or blocks being preferable to avoid wind turbulence.

Natural

a) *Trees*: The White Poplar (*Populus alba*) The Lombardy Poplar (*Populus nigra italia*) *Populus deltoides*

Will eventually form a shelter up to around 40 ft. high and should be planted in double staggered row, 6 to 7 ft. apart between Oct. and March. It should be noted that the roots of Poplars can be a problem.

Thuja occidentalis
Thuja lobbi
Thuja plicata
Pinus Sylvestris
Cupressus macrocarpa (not very hardy)
Cupressocyparis leylandii
Chaemaecyparis lawsoniana

Will all form a tall shelter belt of around 20–30 ft. at least. Plant in September or April 3–5 ft. apart.

b) *Hedges*: Yew (evergreen) Holly (evergreen) Privet (semi-evergreen) Beech: Hornbeam (deciduous) Hawthorn (deciduous)

Will form hedges of 10 ft. or more in height. Privet can pose a problem as far as cutting is concerned. Plant between Oct. and March.

Many gardeners may, of course, have too little space to allow the planting of either hedges or shelter belts, particularly the latter. Garages or dwelling houses, although shutting off some light, will, however, provide a modicum of shelter in all probability.

SOIL CONDITION

Previous reference has been made in Chapter 1 to soil type, and the incidence of pests, diseases and weeds. It has also been said that soil analysis, including a potato eelworm count, is a relatively simple matter in most areas by arrangement with the local advisory service.

The quality of soil and its suitability for crop production is something which has generally to be accepted for better or for worse, and could ultimately decide, in the main, the modes of culture practised. When soil is of good texture and is found, by analysis, to be reasonably well supplied with organic matter and, to a lesser extent, nutrients, then there is every reason to exploit these advantages, and consider the use of the greenhouse borders which will eventually be formed. On the other hand, extremely poor soil conditions such as heavy sticky clay, or, at the other end of the scale, a light sandy gravel, may necessitate growing methods alternative to border culture. It is worth noting, however, that most soils can be improved by liberal applications of peat or other forms of organic matter, especially in the limited area of a greenhouse.

SITE LEVELLING

Flat land is ideal for any type of building, and greenhouses are no exception. Where the slope of the land necessitates levelling, special care is required, particularly when it is intended to use the border soil for cropping, it being essential to leave a reasonable and even depth of top soil. This situation is, of course, different when the house is to be permanently benched. Where top soil is to be retained, levelling procedure should be by one of the following methods, and should preferably be carried out when the soil is fairly dry, to avoid damage to soil texture.

Cut and fill

The top soil is stripped from the site and stacked, levelling being carried out by moving the sub soil from the highest point to the lowest, the top soil then being replaced. This method is ideal for a mild slope, but where a steep slope is involved considerable drainage problems can be encountered unless a retaining wall is built, with a drain behind it to collect shed water from the higher land. Of course where there is a good depth of top soil it may be unnecessary to carry out this procedure in full detail.

Levelling to lowest point

The top soil, if required later, is again stripped and stacked and the sub soil removed to the appropriate level before replacing the top soil. This can also give rise to drainage problems.

Levelling to highest point

I favour this method over the others, especially where the slope is considerable, as it overcomes most drainage problems. The method speaks for itself, as soil or ballast (when border soil is of little account) is used to bring up the level to the appropriate point. A retaining or extended base wall is usually required, coupled, of course, with the necessary quantity of in-fill material. The only real failing of this method is that rapid drainage through the border soil can be a problem, as a large area of the greenhouse is above normal soil level.

It is highly important that whichever method of levelling is used, a suitable time is allowed for soil subsidence before building commences, unless contact can be made with undisturbed soil when erecting the foundations.

ERECTION

Presuming planning permission has been obtained, the next stage is composing the order for the greenhouse. Having had long personal experience with many greenhouse manufacturers, I advise strict attention to detail and precise instructions to avoid errors. Delivery time varies considerably, but in due course the greenhouse will either arrive

Caladiums raised in the greenhouse in pots may be placed outdoors early in June if the weather is warm

A particularly beautiful
chrysanthemum, 'Burning Bronze'

by lorry or by rail, being of course delivered from the station. Always ask for the various sections to be off loaded conveniently for building, but do not clutter up the actual site, this being of some importance as side or roof sections can be heavy. The plans of the greenhouse should then be carefully examined, checking up on measurements, and carefully noting whether 'outside to outside' or 'inside to inside', or 'centre to centre' readings are given. Orientation of the greenhouse will previously have been checked, after due consideration of all the factors involved (see page 11).

The next stage is to peg out the exact position of the greenhouse, using accurately cut 1 in. × 1 in. square pegs, pointed at one end, and 14–16 in. in length, avoiding silly bits of canes. Set one end peg at the decided or specified distance from a fence, building, or other permanent feature, and then, using a good quality steel measuring tape, set out the other end peg, taking into account once again the correct distance from the permanent feature, so that the greenhouse is in line. Some deviation may of course be necessary to adhere to a north/south or east/west orientation, it not being a vital matter if the greenhouse lies a few degrees off in any direction. A reliable compass can be used to check this. It is usual to work from the *centre* of each peg for the correct distance. Now set the levels of these two pegs accurately, or if the house is large an intermediate peg or pegs should be set in also, after stretching a tight line between the two end pegs. 10 or 12 ft. is a convenient distance apart for pegs. While a spirit level and a long straight unwarped board will often suffice to check levels, it is better to borrow a Cowley or 'Dumpy' level for larger houses, provided you know how to use these instruments or can enlist the help of someone who does. It is unlikely that there will be any need to ensure 'run' on a small greenhouse to facilitate movement of rain water, the house being kept completely level, or nearly so. Finally, tap a 2-in. nail lightly into the centre of each peg.

Now comes the difficult task of setting the width of the greenhouse, keeping to an exact right angle. The easiest way is to make up an accurate triangle of pieces of wood, 3, 4 and 5 ft. in length, checking the right angle formed with a joiner's square. Set the corner of this exactly to the nail, supporting the other corners with a brick and, by means of lines, set these exactly along the edges of the triangle to give a right angle. Measuring along the line will then give the breadth, at which point another stake should be inserted. Repeat this procedure at the other corner, checking finally that the distance between the pegs longitudinally is correct. Now level up all the pegs and *tap* a nail into the centre of each corner peg. Alternatively the corner pegs can be set with a builder's site square, which will do the job really accurately, again provided you are shown how to use this instrument really accurately. Now set taut lines exactly to the nails on each corner peg by placing stout pegs 2 to 3 ft. outside the house outline, and remove the corner pegs, as this allows the foundations to be worked on without impediment, particularly at the corners, moving the line out of the way temporarily of course.

FOUNDATIONS
Most greenhouses demand some kind of foundation upon which to build the base wall or set the base blocks, or even merely to attach the base section of the house to, and the requisite method will always be specified by the supplier. Do-it-yourself enthusiasts building a complete greenhouse will usually be fairly competent in any case, and the necessary foundations should not offer them any problem. It is highly important to realise that firm anchorage to the ground is essential. When a full 9 in. brick wall is contemplated, take out a trench 5 to 6 in. deep and 12 to 14 in. across, in the appropriate place, with deference to precisely what the set line denotes (generally the outside edge of the *greenhouse* structure). There may well be special requirements in this respect to extend the wall beyond the sill plate of the greenhouse. Half brick (4½ in.) walls, composition block walls, or special base blocks will require a trench of the same depth, but 8 to 9 in. wide. Deeper trenches may be necessary to contact undisturbed soil where levelling has recently taken place.

The foundation should consist of concrete of approximately 3 parts finely broken brick, 2 parts rough sand and 1 part cement (all by bulk), run in in a 4 to 5 in. deep layer, or perhaps deeper as directed by the greenhouse plans, and 'dumped' fairly level with a straight board. Any securing bolts should, if necessary, be set in at the appropriate point when running in the foundations, again by observing directions. After a suitable period to allow the foundations to harden, brick or block building can proceed, using a 3:1 sand/cement mixture (by bulk), again adhering strictly to the plans to ensure that the base wall placement is consistent in relation to greenhouse size. Due allowance for doors or box ventilators must be made as building proceeds. It is highly important that the wall or blocks run true and plumb, as checked frequently with a spirit level and a plumb bob. If the base wall is especially high, reinforcing with piles may be advisable, this often being the case on sloping sites.

BUILDING PROCEDURE
This will vary considerably according to the design of the greenhouse. Usually full instructions are supplied, and with large prefabricated sections there are few difficulties. Glazing methods vary from old-fashioned putty and nails to plastic strip and clip, the latter now generally being used in all aluminium alloy houses. Sealing strips and non-hardening bitumen are also becoming very popular. Dry glazed Dutch light type greenhouses offer no glazing problems at all, as the glass slides into grooves. Always try to glaze when the glass and astragals are dry.

5 Greenhouse maintenance

While modern types of greenhouse structures require the very minimum of attention, there are some chores which cannot be avoided.

PAINTING AND TREATING

Wooden greenhouses constructed of hardwoods such as oak or teak require little or no treatment to remain in good condition, although they can get oiled occasionally. Red Cedar, although not requiring painting either, should also be treated with linseed oil every few years. Soft woods, if pressure treated, will last for a long time without any painting, although their appearance is sometimes uninspiring in this condition. Untreated soft woods require regular painting. White lead paint should be used on top of a priming coat or, if the wood is clean or cleaned with a wire brush, aluminium paint is useful, but not generally as attractive or long lasting as white lead paint. Where putty is used, it is usual to paint over this and extend the paintwork $\frac{1}{8}$—$\frac{1}{16}$ in. over the glass to give a good seal. A piece of thin metal of the right size is useful to prevent painting over too much of the glass, but at best it is still an extremely time demanding task. Painting both the outside and inside of greenhouses definitely improves light transmission by reflection, apart from general appearance. Spirit based preservatives can be used in lieu of paint, but I feel that this is a task to be carried out before the house is built, especially a do-it-yourself type, and particularly for the wooden structural members of plastic greenhouses. However, it costs so little to have the wood pressure treated with preservative before purchase, that it is often better to adopt this course of action. Benches and shelves inside the house should certainly be initially treated with a spirit-based preservative, even if eventually painted. Creosote, while an excellent wood preservative, should *not* be used for greenhouses or benches, owing to the damaging fumes which are given off, especially when heat is applied. Alloy and metal houses require no painting, although some steel houses may require painting in time, preferably with aluminium paint.

CLEANING THE GLASS

Gardeners perhaps do not appreciate how much the light transmission qualities of glass are reduced by dirt adhering to it, both inside and out, especially in suburbia. It takes but a little time to clean the outside of the glass with either a proprietary glass cleaner or a solution of oxalic acid, 1 lb. to 1 gal. of water, sprayed on the glass and washed off with a hose pipe. For the inside of the glass any good detergent will suffice when it is possible to empty the greenhouse temporarily to allow this. Moss and algae which lodges on the edges and overlaps of glass must be physically dislodged, although the treatment described above will take care of most deposits on the outside. A piece of thin metal, in association with a strong jet of water, will clean the overlap, but usually only physical removal will take care of moss on the outside and inside, in certain positions. Moss is much more prone to develop on the north side of the greenhouse. In some areas it is sometimes necessary, after a few years, to completely re-glaze certain types of houses, especially those which do not have a 'barcap' fitting to seal the glass and astragal completely.

The use of aluminium covered glazing strip has much to commend it where it is desired to avoid conventional re-glazing.

CLEANING BASE WALLS
The base walls inside should be given a good scrub annually, and preferably whitewashed. Heating pipes should be given a coat of aluminium paint occasionally, this apparently not having the detrimental effect on heat transmission once thought to be the case.

6 Heating systems for greenhouses

There is, in many ways, the same basic similarity between greenhouse and domestic heating. One hears so much about the efficiency of the different methods that confusion is inevitable. Yet the artificial heating of any building is a precise science, and the cost and efficiency of every method can be readily calculated. Perhaps the real truth is that although accurate information is available on heating systems from many sources, many people do not take the time to assimilate it properly, or are too readily swayed by lavish National advertising.

SOME VARIABLE FACTORS

There are, nevertheless, quite a few variable factors to be considered. All materials have a conductivity factor which allows the passage of heat in both directions. Glass is a good transmitter of heat and this indeed is why it is so effective in allowing the passage of solar heat. Glass, therefore, is a poor insulator and while it can, unlike many plastics, effectively trap the reflected long heat waves, it cannot store heat for long, which means that when the outside temperature drops below the temperature of the greenhouse, heat will readily flow back through the glass. Reduce the area of glass and heat loss is reduced accordingly, as also is solar heat transmission, a matter which has already been referred to. Increase the wind speed on the outside surface of the glass, and loss of heat is still more rapid. Allow air spaces below or around doors, badly fitting ventilators, or glass, and the heat loss is still further increased, this time by the physical loss of heated air, and the entry of cooler air.

Double glazing is effective in a dwelling house because two layers of glass, hermetically sealed, trap an insulating blanket of dead air between them. Double glazed greenhouses are also available or can be constructed, but these are costly. A crude form of double glazing is to line the inside of a greenhouse with polythene, leaving the ventilators free of course, and while this can be effective to a degree, it gives rise to excessive humidity unless ventilation is particularly effective, as it can be with extractor fans. (See also page 50.)

CALCULATION OF HEAT LOSS

Heating engineers always start their appraisal of any heating project by calculating the heat loss of the building concerned.

They do this by assuming an accepted figure for the thermal conductivity of various materials. These are approximately:

	Per sq. ft. per hour, per degree
Glass (including its framework)	1.1 BTU per hour (British Thermal Unit)
4½ in. brick wall or composition block	.5 BTU per hour
Double brick wall, 9 in.	.4 BTU per hour
Wood 1 in. thick	.5 BTU per hour
Asbestos (sheet or corrugated)	1.1 BTU per hour (approx)
Concrete 4 in. thick	.75 BTU per hour
Double glazed glass (properly sealed)	.5 BTU per hour
Polythene lining (see page 38).	

Note: There is also technically a heat loss through the floor or ground of the greenhouse, but in practice this is frequently ignored, as the ground area of a greenhouse is often a very effective storage medium for heat, throwing this back into the greenhouse.

To make use of these figures for the purpose of calculation, it is necessary to measure up the total areas in square feet, and this is quite a simple matter. It is better to draw a plan and append the necessary measurements to this. The brick base walls (if any), the total area of glass, and the ends are all measured up and the areas multiplied by the appropriate figure. (See Fig. 2.)

ARRIVING AT THE NECESSARY HEAT INPUT

The figure of 259 BTUs is the heat loss of a perfectly tight greenhouse, which is an unusual occurrence. Normally there are leaks and one must also take into account the effect of exposure. Generally one third is added to allow for these additional losses, although this figure could be much greater in a very exposed situation, and *less* in a very sheltered position with a very tight greenhouse. Assuming an addition of one third, the figure of 259 becomes 343 BTUs. The decision must now be made as to what level of heating is required. This will depend on region, and of course on the type of cultivation intended. A greenhouse to be maintained at 65°F. in all weathers would require a 45–50°F. 'lift' over the outside temperature, assuming that it could be as low as 20°F. out of doors. Therefore to calculate the heat input the figure of 343 is multiplied by 45 or 50. Generally speaking for a temperate or intermediate house a 35°F. lift is allowed, and for the cool house a 20°–25°F. lift. Assuming an intermediate house temperature is the aim, the figure of 343 is multiplied by 35 and therefore becomes 12,005, which is the heat requirement figure in BTUs no matter what type of heating system is involved. For W/metre square Degree C × 5.6.

TYPES OF HEATING SYSTEMS

To maintain an acceptable temperature range throughout the year in a greenhouse in Britain, some form of artificial heat is necessary. There have been rapid developments in heating methods during recent years and further progress can certainly be expected. The emphasis is on entirely automatic, or at least semi-automatic, systems which absolve the gardener from any work or worry, although not all gardeners are prepared to pay for this level of sophistication, at the outset at any rate. There are many different ways of heating a greenhouse, or sections of it, i.e. the border soil or propagating bench. The following are the main methods:
1 By an arrangement of water-containing pipes, the water being heated initially by a boiler 'fired' with solid fuel, oil, gas or electricity. Simple types of solid fuel boilers cannot be considered automatic, whereas more refined types operate with ease on a semi-automatic control system. There is no control problem at all with more refined oil, gas or electric boilers. Electricity also is of course required for the operation of the majority of automatic types.

2 Oil heaters with either free discharge or ducted heated air. These can be of either simple design, such as oil stoves, or with pressure jet or vapouriser burners, with or without assisted air discharge by means of fans. Electricity is again required for pressure jet burners, and the operation of fans. Simple types of oil heaters must be controlled manually,

whereas all other types, provided they are controlled electrically, can be operated on a thermostat (see also page 48).

3 Entirely by electrical apparatus in various forms, all of which are ideal for automatic control.

    a) *Soil or bench warming cables* which have little effect on the greenhouse air temperature.

    b) *Mineral insulated (M.I.) cables* for installation around the greenhouse perimeter, these being held in porcelain clips.

    c) *Tubular heaters* of various sizes and designs which are generally fitted on perimeter walls.

    d) *Fan heaters* which can be sited anywhere, but are generally freestanding in the centre of the greenhouse, unless of course they are the larger type fan heaters which can be sited at one end of the house, the hot air being distributed by perforated polythene ducts, as also can be done with oil fired fan heaters.

    e) *Storage heaters*. Opinions vary concerning the use of these in a greenhouse owing to problems of temperature control.

COST OF OPERATING VARIOUS SYSTEMS

This depends on many factors, apart from the basic cost of the fuel. The main factors are the desired heat level and the percentage efficiency of the heat producing unit as, with all systems of heating involving combustion, there is always a proportion of heat wasted, generally into the atmosphere through the flue pipe. Although freestanding oil heaters have no outside flue, there is still an efficiency loss on combustion. Fuel supplying bodies are generally happy to provide reasonably accurate average running costs, based broadly on the general principles stated here.

DISTRIBUTION OF HEAT

Another important matter relates to the distribution of heat once it is produced, it being desirable to design a system which will give an equable and even heat dispersal throughout the whole greenhouse area, especially for heat demanding crops in cold weather. Hot water pipe systems are ideal, as they can provide a warm curtain around the outside of the

TYPE OF SYSTEM	AVERAGE OPERATIONAL EFFICIENCY	APPROX. RUNNING COSTS PER 100,000 B.T.U's. (Therm) at fuel prices as stated.
Solid fuel boiler of simple design. Hard coal.	50%	Based on coal at 12,500 BTU's per cwt. Cost of fuel per cwt. 15/– = 1/11d. per therm 14/– = 1/9d. ,, 13/– = 1/8d. ,, 12/– = 1/6d. ,,
More refined solid fuel boiler using smokeless fuel or coke	60%	Based on a value of 12,000 BTU's/lb. Cost of fuel per cwt. 15/– = 1/10½d. per therm 14/– = 1/9d. ,, 13/– = 1/7d. ,,
	70%	15/– = 1/7d. ,, 14/– = 1/6d. ,, 13/– = 1/4½d. ,,
Purpose-made oil fired boiler and fan heaters with external flue (some types have no flue and this results in slightly higher operational efficiency)	75%	Based on oil at 162,000 BTU's per gallon Cost of fuel per gall.(Bulk purchase. Small quantities can be approx. 25% more) 1/6d. = 1/3d. per therm 1/5d. = 1/2d. ,, 1/4d. = 1/1d. ,, 1/3d. = 1/–d. ,, 1/2d. = 11½d. ,,
Converted oil fired boiler with vaporiser type burner (Figures for free-standing oil heaters are fairly similar but are generally more advantageous in respect of running costs only)	70%	Based on oil at 158,000 BTU's per gallon Cost of fuel per gall. (Remarks on bulk purchase again apply) 1/7d. = 1/5d. per therm 1/6d. = 1/4d. ,, 1/5d. = 1/3d. ,, 1/4d. = 1/2½d. ,, 1/3d. = 1/1½d. ,,
Purpose-made gas fired boiler	75–80%	Based on actual cost of gas per therm, which varies considerably according to district, less 20–25% for loss of efficiency.
All types of electrical heaters (Residual heat from storage heaters is considerable and is difficult to allow for in comparative tables. Off-peak tarriffs are usually lower than those stated here, but cannot be considered for)	100%	Based on normal tarriff [*] Cost per unit 2d. = 4/10d. per therm 1.3d. = 3/2d. ,, 1.25d. = 3/– ,, 1.2d. = 2/11d. ,, 1.15d. = 2/9d. ,, 1.1d. = 2/8d. ,,

[*] Primary unit costs should be allowed for

After 15th February 1971 convert to decimal currency

42

greenhouse. They transmit the heat largely by convection currents, as hot air rises. Heating can be most efficient, provided the pipes are maintained at the same temperature throughout their length. The pipes also transmit a considerable amount of radiant heat, which can be valuable for soil warming purposes where heat-loving crops such as tomatoes are involved, and also for many plant growing and propagation activities on benches.

Non-directional heaters of any type merely transmit their heat entirely by convection and consequently are not considered as ideal for uniform heat distribution, especially in very cold weather or where cold winds prevail along one side of the greenhouse. Directional heaters with fans are more efficient, but there can also be distribution problems unless perforated polythene ducting is employed to disperse the heated air uniformly around the greenhouse.

Heating engineers and equipment suppliers are well aware of the need for good design with any heating system, and a wealth of good advice is also available from the advisory bodies associated with all fuel suppliers.

SMALL BORE SYSTEMS

Small diameter pipe systems contain less water than 4-in. pipe systems, a $1\frac{1}{4}$-in. system requiring only one fifth of the volume of water of a 4-in. system of similar BTU capacity. There must, of course, be a longer length of $1\frac{1}{4}$ in. piping. This means that much less water has to be heated initially, but of course the system cools more quickly. This, however, ensures a much better and more accurate response to changing temperatures, and this is the main reason why commercial growers now never install the 4-in. pipe system, which was commercial practice for many years. However, when a long length of small bore system is required to obtain the necessary heat input, circulation may be difficult due to the higher frictional resistance of small diameter pipes as compared to larger ones, and a circulating pump may therefore be required. Hot water filled pipes emit heat at the following level per foot run at a 100°F. temperature difference (the difference between the temperature of the water in the pipe and the air temperature.)

43

1 in.	80 B.T.U's	
1¼ in.	100 ,,	
1½ in.	110 ,,	To nearest
2 in.	130 ,,	
2½ in.	150 ,,	round
3 in.	190 ,,	
3½ in.	200 ,,	figures
4 in.	230 ,,	

To find out the appropriate length of piping in feet (see page 46), divide the figure given above into the total heat load for the greenhouse in question, arrived at by calculation.

DESIGN PROCEDURE
To make matters still more simple, the following is the sequence of operations for designing a heating system for the average greenhouse. First of all calculate the heat loss of the greenhouse, and after deciding on the desired temperature range, calculate the total heat loss in BTUs, adding one third or more, according to the estimated exposure of the district. It is common practice also to provide for a certain reserve when designing a system.

It is now always advisable to check with the operating costs table the cost of running each system, it being usual to allow for a 50 to 60% demand on the system. Presume, for example, that one was interested in installing an electrical fan system and the heat load was, as calculated earlier, 12,005 BTUs. 1 Kw. of electricity is 3,412 BTUs, which means that the greenhouse system must be designed to give this amount of heat, i.e. $\frac{12005}{3412} = 3\frac{1}{2}$ Kw. approximately. Referring to the chart, it costs 3/– for 100,000 BTUs at 1.25 pence per unit. 100,000 BTUs would supply approximately 8½ hours of heat at full output of the heating appliance (the heat loss of the greenhouse being 12,005 BTUs per hour), which, in round figures is about 8/6d. per day. The necessity for full continuous output is highly unlikely, however, unless the weather is exceptionally cold, a 50 to 60% demand being reasonable, which means around 4/– to 5/– per day. Similarly, for an oil fired boiler at 75% efficiency and fuel at 1/6d. per gallon it costs 1/3d. per therm, and this would again supply 8½ hours cf heating at full output, which means approximately 3/6d. per day. At 50 to 60% demand this figure decreases to around 2/– per day. One can carry out endless calculations along these lines. I feel that it is very obvious that electrical heating for greenhouses is costly where high temperatures have to be maintained, and is only 'economic' where a 'cool' greenhouse is involved and a 45°F. minimum temperature is the aim. The real bonus with electricity is, of course, the complete lack of supervision and maintenance, and many gardeners are therefore prepared to meet the extra cost involved. Although running costs are high, however, installation costs are generally low.

SELECTING A HEATING SYSTEM

Armed with the operational economics of the various systems, the next stage is to select the type of heating best suited for the purpose. I think one must accept that pipe systems, whether oil, solid fuel or gas fired, are the most economic to run, and in more or less the order stated, a lot depending on the actual cost of the fuel. In many ways there is very little to choose between solid fuel and oil in an efficient boiler, but one would have to take into account the labour content of solid fuel firing as compared to semi or completely automatic firing with oil, according to the level of sophistication one is prepared to pay for. Pipe and boiler systems are, however, costly to install initially, and the cost will be more or less pro-rata according to the degree of refinement desired. The cheapest form of oil burner, as distinct from oil stoves, is the vaporising type installed either in a steel or cast iron boiler (Fig. 5). Installation must be carefully carried out to ensure maximum utilisation of the hot gasses, this being achieved by baffling the flames on to the side of the boiler and by ensuring that with the natural draught type vaporiser, the flue draught is reduced to the very minimum by the fitting of a draught diverter, or removing a suitably placed soot cleaning plate.

SITING OF BOILER

Any boiler should, of course, always be sited to the side away from the prevailing wind so that the flue gases do not constantly stain the glass. Boilers can either be inside the greenhouse or, more preferably, in a small boiler house constructed on the north side of the greenhouse. This ensures a more steady draught and higher efficiency with any type of fuel, as the boiler is protected from wind.

PIPE LAYOUT

Pipe layout in greenhouses can vary greatly according to pipe diameter and whether or not a circulating pump is installed in the system. Generally speaking all pipe systems must be designed so that there is a gradual rise of at least 1 in. in 10 ft. to the highest part in the system, at which point there is either an expansion tank or a breather valve. This allows the system to operate on what is known as the thermo-syphon principle, where hot water rises because it is less dense than cold water. There should also be a drain cock on the boiler or return pipe at the lowest point so that the system, when not in operation, can be fully drained in cold weather to avoid frost damage. The usual place for pipes is on the perimeter wall to provide the warm curtain of heat referred to earlier. On the other hand, some gardeners prefer pipes under their benches for propagation purposes, and this also can easily be allowed for.

Thermo-syphon systems are more successful when large diameter pipes are used, but as stated earlier, these pipes are now more or less obsolete in commercial spheres, the small diameter now being standard, as are circulating pumps. This means that it is not necessary to follow too exactly any precise pipe levels, as the water will be pumped round independent of any rises or falls in the pipe system, thus enabling much more flexibility in design and placement of the pipes in the most convenient situation. Flexible rubber couplings can be used in lieu of screwed bends or joints, and are ideal for a pipe system which can be modified according to crop needs. Pipes can be used under benches for propagation, then dropped to ground level when the benches are removed to plant a crop of tomatoes (Fig. 6). This has many advantages, especially as it provides excellent soil warming and evenly dispersed heat for a warmth-loving crop such as tomatoes. *Whatever design is adopted, provision must always be made for drawing off the water completely during frosty weather.*

There are obviously many different designs possible with pipe systems, and it is often better to seek the advice of a competent heating engineer or horticultural adviser, to obtain general guidance before proceeding too far.

COST OF HEATING SYSTEMS

The cost of installing a heating system will vary enormously, according not only to the heat level desired, but to the type of system and whether it has to be automatic or manual. Obviously, too, employing tradesmen to instal a pipe system will be a lot more costly than self-installation. The following is a very approximate guide to costs (1971):

Oil Stoves – £4–£8.

Tubular heaters – (electric) – From £2 per 2 ft. unit to £9 for a treble 6 ft. unit.

Fan Heaters (electric) – £9–£10 for $1\frac{1}{2}$ Kw, £12 for $2\frac{1}{2}$ Kw, £15 for 3 Kw, £23 for $4\frac{1}{2}$ Kw.

$1\frac{1}{4}''$ steel piping (medium grade) is approximately $7\frac{1}{2}$p to $8\frac{1}{2}$p per foot.

Circulating pumps cost around £12–£15.

Boilers vary greatly and prices should be sought from a heating engineer.

Small second-hand domestic boilers can frequently be used at considerable savings.

SOME USEFUL INSTALLATION HINTS

It has been stated that boilers should always be sited on the windward side of the greenhouse so that fumes are invariably carried away by wind. Note, however, that flue pipes should not constitute a hazard for your own or your neighbours' dwelling house or greenhouse. Flue chimneys should, if possible, be above the highest point of the greenhouse.

While it is common practice to use the structure of the greenhouse for securing heating pipes, remember that these are heavy and could cause damage to a flimsy structure, especially those greenhouses with sloping sides. It is better to make up special pipe supports if there is the least doubt.

Fuel tanks for oil burners should be sited as conveniently as possible, and preferably in a position which does not shut off valuable sunlight. The outlet of the tank should be at least 12 to 15 in. above the level of the burner, or at the appropriate level indicated by burner manufacturers. An old 40-gallon oil drum with a breather fitted will often suffice.

When circulating pumps are installed in small bore heating systems, make sure that the water supply tank is sited sufficiently high above the circulating head of the pump to avoid the syphoning out of water through the supply tank and the creation of a vacuum in the system, which can cause considerable damage. Advice on these matters must be sought from a qualified heating engineer or the pump manufacturer.

Only use rubber hose pipe of superior quality for bends and couplings with small bore systems, and make sure that the expanding clips used are in first class order, and tight. Breathers at highest points may not always be necessary where rubber couplings are used, as it is a simple matter to loosen the appropriate couplings to let air out.

If threaded pipes of smaller diameter are used to allow the fitting of bends, joints, etc., always use a *good* jointing paste.

Boilers vary considerably in design and it is always advisable to take time to read the installation and operating instructions carefully.

CONTROL OF HEAT INPUT
It is impossible to separate the control of heat input from ventilation and other environmental control factors, as the whole subject tends to be complex. Many gardeners are, however, merely concerned with the effective control of their heating appliance according to the temperature requirement of the greenhouse, as measured by thermometer reading.

All electrical equipment is the essence of simplicity with regard to control (see however notes which follow on storage heaters) and undoubtedly this is why it is so popular for the 'cool' greenhouse requiring frost protection and little else. The appliance may be linked to a thermostat, if in fact one is not already built into it in the first case, although in the

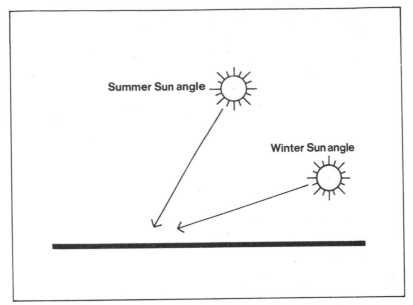

Fig. 1 The angle of the incidence of the sun varies
considerably between winter and summer (see page 18).

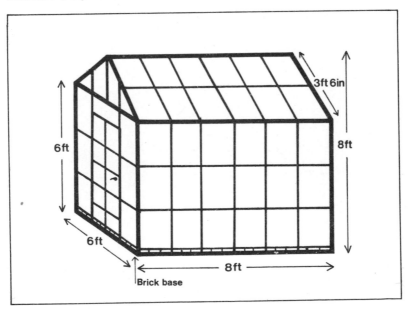

Fig. 2 The all-glass greenhouse (see page 39).

Sides:	2 x 8′ x 6′	=(48 x 2) 96 sq. ft.
Ends:	2 x 6′ x 6′	=(36 x 2) 72 sq. ft.
Roof:	2 x 8′ x 3′6″	=(28 x 2) 56 sq. ft.
Gable ends:	2 x 3′ x 2′	=(6 x 2) 12 sq. ft.

The calculation shows 236 sq. ft. with a heat
loss of 1.1 BTUs per square foot =259 BTUs.

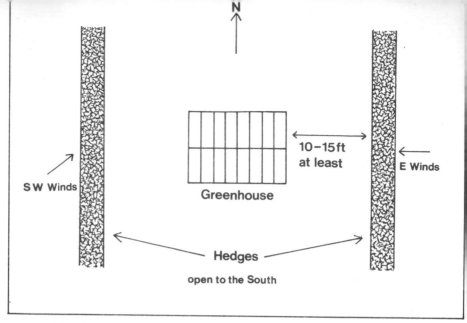

N

S W Winds

E Winds

Greenhouse

10–15ft
at least

Hedges

open to the South

Fig. 3 *(above)* Sheltering the greenhouse (see page 29).
Fig. 4 *(below)* The ground area of a greenhouse is often
a very effective storage medium for heat (see page 39).

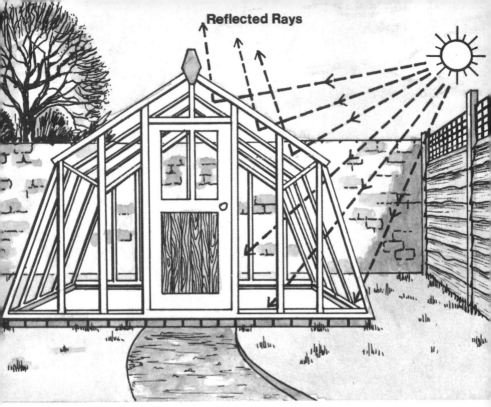

Reflected Rays

Fig. 4A The conventional sloping roof of
a span-roofed greenhouse, with its length
orientated east-west, deflects winter sunlight.

Fig. 5 Vaporising type of burner (see page 45).
Maximum use of hot gases is
achieved by baffling the flames.

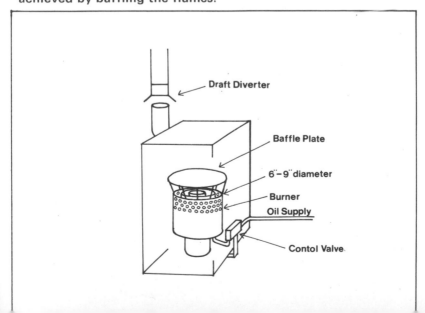

Draft Diverter

Baffle Plate

6"–9" diameter

Burner

Oil Supply

Contol Valve

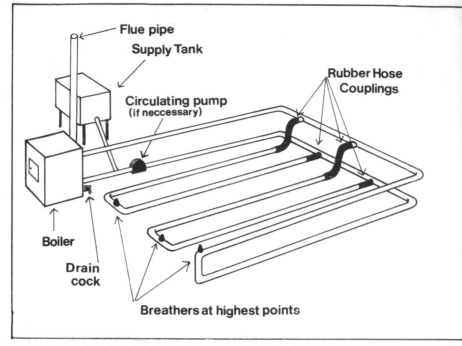

Fig. 6 Showing flexible rubber couplings to allow pipe movement (see page 46).

Fig. 7 Low-pressure steam steriliser (see page 73).

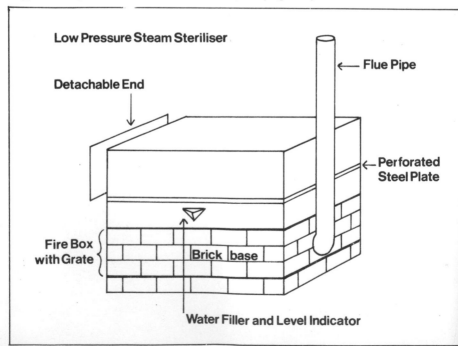

Picture 8 Standard chrysanthemums must be
disbudded to get large single blooms

Picture 9 Inserting cuttings round edge of a clay
pot ensures maximum air and warmth

Picture 10 Good shape is essential for quality cucumbers

Picture 11 *Peperomia magnoliaefolia*

Picture 12 Tomatoes ready for pricking off

Picture 13 *Pilea cadiena*

Picture 14 A young chrysanthemum after its first potting

Picture 15 A small lean-to greenhouse built against the wall of a dwelling house

Picture 16 Cacti: *Aeonium arborescens cristata* *Scottish Field*

Picture 18 Cacti: *Notactus leninghausii cristata*   *Scottish Field*

Picture 19 Chrysanthemum: *'Delaware' (yellow)*   *Scottish Field*

Picture 20 *Hydrangea hortensia* — *Scottish Field*

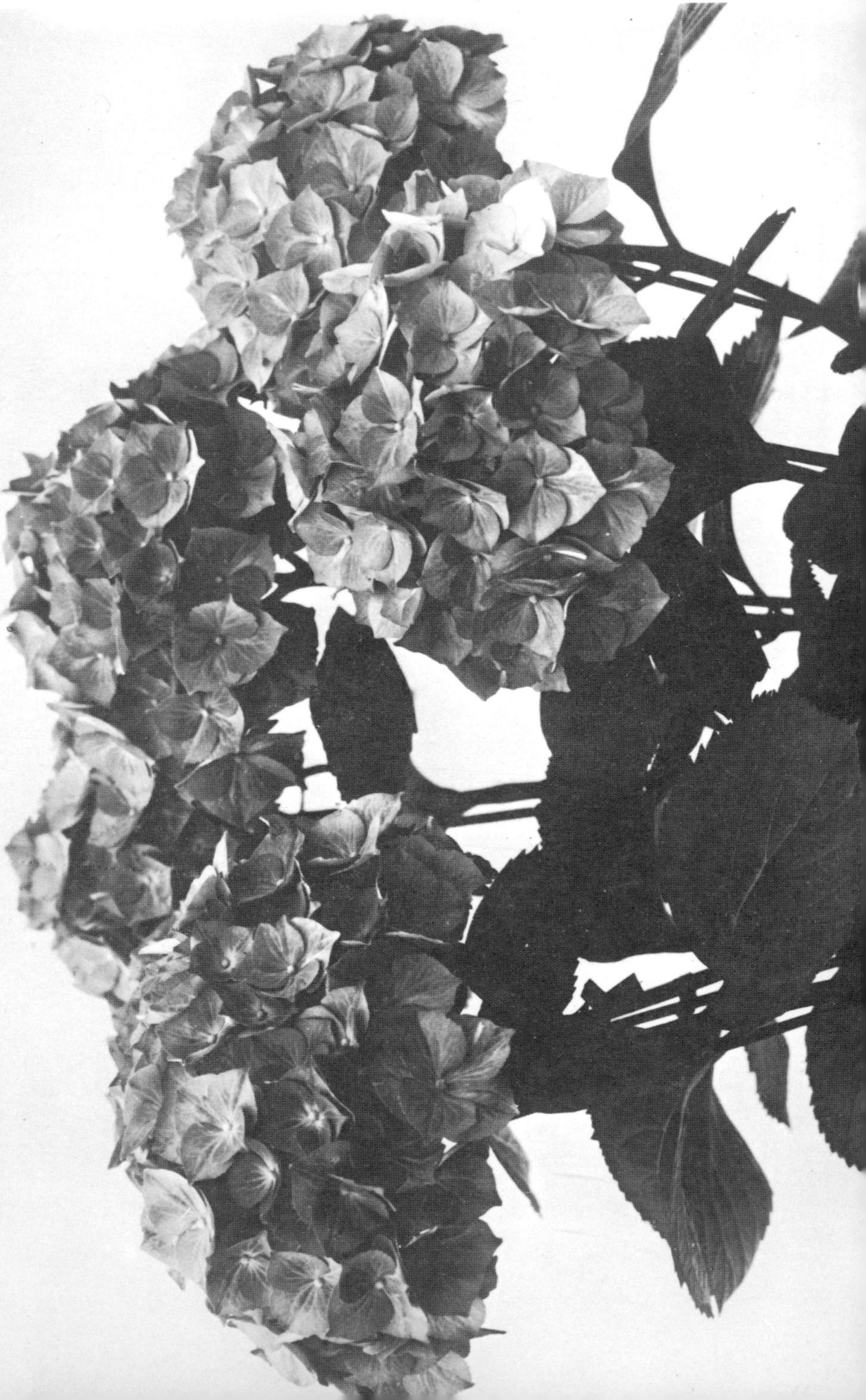

Picture 21 Hydrangea massed under glass   *Scottish Field*

interests of accuracy the former state of affairs is to be preferred.

Simple oil-fired stoves require to be manually lit and extinguished, and their effectiveness in maintaining an even temperature depends on efficient and constant attention. The same is true of most solid fuel boilers linked to pipe systems, except those of more refined design, especially where the distribution of heat through the pipe system occurs as soon as the boiler is in operation, as is generally the case when circulation of water depends entirely on gravity circulation. The same may be said of simple oil-fired boiler gravity circulating systems, these being common where vaporiser burners are used, although thermostatic expansion type controls can be linked to cut the burner to a pilot flame, and this gives the same degree of flexibility possible where thermostatic flue regulators are fitted on solid fuel boilers.

Refined gas and oil-fired boilers present no control problems, as the boiler can be called into action through a thermostat set in the greenhouse.

Where, however, a small bore pipe system depends *entirely* on the operation of a circulating pump (in other words where there is no gravity circulation at all), excellent control can be achieved by linking a greenhouse sited thermostat to the pump. The boiler can therefore be left to maintain its own temperature, as dictated by either manual or automatic firing, and is constantly poised ready to supply heat. This type of control system is *not advisable for cast iron pipe systems* due to the damage which may be caused to pipes and joints by sudden expansion. Solenoid valves can also be used to give a similar type of control.

CONSERVATORIES OR PORCHES LINKED TO DOMESTIC SYSTEMS

Off-peak storage electric heaters in conservatories or porches which are part of the domestic heating system will merely be controllable within the limits of their design. If of the simple on/off type, there can be considerable control problems. A warm day following a cold night when the storage heater has been in operation will result in excess heat and the use of ventilators, especially when solar heat input is high. A controllable input/output system of off-peak storage heating is the only real answer, although even this system still gives rise to difficulties in a glass structure, as opposed to a conventional building, due to solar heat input. A much more frequent arrangement is to link conservatories and porches to a domestic small bore hot water system. Control problems can also exist here, especially if the domestic system is operated by a time clock which puts the whole system out of action overnight. If, however, the boiler is maintained at operating temperature, both to prevent low temperature corrosion and provide constant hot water, and the domestic system only on time clock control is linked to a circulating pump, a separate pump can be used for the conservatory or porch. Alternatively, thermostatic valves can be used, provided circulation can be ensured to the conservatory or porch without calling the house system into operation. Hot air ducted systems of heating offer similar control problems. Such matters are best taken up with a qualified heating engineer, preferably when the system is initially installed.

POLYTHENE LINING OF GREENHOUSES

This is common practice nowadays and is effective in reducing heat loss, and consequently in saving fuel. Wooden houses lend themselves better to the tacking on of thin grade polythene (150 gauge) to the sides of the greenhouse astragals, leaving the vents clear. Metal houses are much more difficult to double glaze, and it is necessary to use a light wooden frame or other convenient method. Humidity in the greenhouse is increased considerably with polythene lining, but this can be an advantage for early season propagation work. Entry of light is not greatly restricted by the polythene.

7 Ventilation and shading

Warm air, being lighter than cool air, rises, which facilitates ventilation and therefore lowering of the temperature. This is simply effected in a greenhouse by allowing air heated by solar radiation or artificial means to escape out of vents set at a suitable point, generally (but not always) in the highest part of the structure. As the hot air escapes, cooler air is drawn in through the vents from outside by reciprocal interchange, or under pressure by wind or breeze. It is also drawn in through overlaps of glass, cracks below doors, and other places, as few glasshouses are by any means airtight. The rate at which this air change takes place depends mainly on the size and position of the ventilators. If cooler air can also be introduced from lower set ventilators, the speed of air change is generally increased considerably, manually operated louvre type vents now becoming popular for this purpose.

Green plants require a constant supply of carbon dioxide during daylight if they are to manufacture foodstuffs in their leaves by the process of photosynthesis. Unless air change takes place, therefore, the supply of carbon dioxide can become depleted, especially during very hot sunny weather when the rate of photosynthesis is high. A further important facet of ventilation, especially for the prevention or restriction of disease, is the reduction of humidity. This is effected under most conditions by the discharge of the warmer moist air and its replacement with cooler outside air of lower humidity.

It has earlier been stated that the effective ventilation area of a greenhouse should be one fifth to one sixth of the floor area for commercial blocks of greenhouses if they are to qualify for Government grant aid, but I would feel that this ratio is on the low side for the smaller amateur greenhouse, which has a larger solar radiation input in relation to total size than a commercial block of glasshouses.

FAN VENTILATION
As distinct from what might be called 'conventional' ventila-

tion, extractor fan systems, capable of giving 50 or 60 air changes per hour, are excellent, but the fan speed should be low to avoid excessive air speeds, otherwise plants may be retarded in growth, or even damaged. This means using larger diameter slow speed fans in preference to those generally used in domestic circles. The fans should be louvred to prevent unwanted air entry when the fans are not in operation, and there should also be a sufficient inlet for air at the opposite end or side of the greenhouse, the ratio of this depending largely on the size and efficiency of the fan. A time clock is also useful for intermittent night operation. This is information readily available from the fan manufacturer.

AIR CONDITIONING
Pressurised or 'air conditioning' system are also now available and work on the principle of pushing cooler outside air into the house, to be expelled either through leaks in the structure, by counterbalanced plastic louvres which open when air pressure rises to a certain point, or some form of automatic means. A mist nozzle, operated by a humidistat, wets the in-coming air when the humidity drops below the desired level. Heaters can also be incorporated in this arrangement. In all cases the operation of the fan is controlled by a thermostat, preferably aspirated (see page 54). A time clock is a useful device for period operation of the fans during the night in summer to prevent excessive humidity.

Conventional ventilators can be opened automatically on thermostat operation by a variety of means. Entirely electrical systems which pull the vents open by cables, or alternatively thermostatically controlled winders, are attractive for the amateur size greenhouse, as opposed to the many different commercial types of actuators. Non-electrical expansion type ventilator lifts are extremely useful and reasonably accurate in practice. They are cheap too. There is, therefore, no need to accept purely manual ventilators in any greenhouse today, due to the low cost of making at least part of the operation automatic, leaving perhaps some supplementary ventilators to be opened manually during very hot weather.

SHADING OF GREENHOUSES

By restricting the input of solar radiation it is possible to reduce the level of heat in a greenhouse, and this may be desirable for many pot plants, early propagation, and numerous other activities. An attack of Verticillium wilt on tomatoes may also necessitate shading (see page 156). Physical restriction of the sun can be achieved by the use of slatted or roller plastic blinds, preferably shaded green, either inside the greenhouse or on wooden frames out of doors. This allows shading to be used merely when necessary. Painting the outside of the glass with a mixture of lime and water, plus a little size, will serve admirably, as the whiteness reflects, instead of absorbing the sunlight. This is particularly effective on the south facing side. Proprietary green coloured shading material can also be used. In both cases the shading generally washes off during the course of the summer, and any which remains can be brushed off before the winter months, when all available sunlight is desirable.

8 Accurate environmental control

As has already been stated, there are three main facets of temperature control, 1, to control the amount of artificial heat input, 2, ventilation (see also page 51) to expel hot air from the greenhouse and allow the entry of cool fresh air from outside, 3, control of humidity – all of which are becoming increasingly dependent on accurate controlling instruments. One vital issue concerned with heat input, ventilation, humidity or any form of environmental control, is to avoid relying on openly sited thermometers or other instruments. Solar heat absorption by the surface of the instruments, radiation loss at night, and the chilling or up-setting effect of draughts are likely to result in erratic behaviour by all types of controlling instruments. The ordinary open sited thermostat will be the most common instrument in amateur greenhouses, with the result that heat may be called for or ventilating systems put into operation at complete variance to the actual air temperature of the greenhouse. An openly sited thermometer is also completely unreliable as a means of measuring heat level under varying conditions.

ASPIRATED SCREENS
A first class investment for the enthusiastic gardener is an aspirated screen. This usually takes the form of a metal box lined with insulating material or a section of large diameter P.V.C. tubing, air inlet being provided through a close mesh screen. A small fan is installed in the screen to provide a constant flow of air over the controlling instruments. If the screen is situated at the level of plant growth, the controlling instruments therefore respond to air temperatures or humidity which are fully representative of that adjacent to the growing plants. An aspirated screen is therefore ideal for heating systems of all types operated on a thermostat, and the same is true of those ventilating systems dependent on electricity, such as fans or electrically controlled vent gear (see Chapter 7). Much more sophisticated control gear, responding to light intensity, is now available to give the operation of heating and/or ventilating in stages and, where CO_2 enrichment is practiced, the shutting of ventilators for the enrichment period.

Integrating photometers are also now available which adjust temperature level, heat input, or ventilator operation, according to the prevailing light intensity, the highly developed forms of these instruments taking into account the precise pattern of preceeding weather, to avoid subjecting plants to 'check' periods, as will be the case when several dull days are followed by excessively bright weather.

THERMOMETERS AND OTHER INSTRUMENTS
It is important to measure temperature accurately, and a good thermometer should always be selected. A maximum/

minimum thermometer is still the best tool for the average gardener. Hygrometers for humidity measurement are not likely to appeal to many gardeners, but are available. A wealth of technical information on all these aspects can be obtained by contacting the firms manufacturing the equipment.

HUMIDITY CONTROL
Humidity (the level of moisture vapour in the atmosphere) has a vital role to play in plant growth, and humidistats can be used either to ventilate or call for heat, also to put in operation mist nozzles in an air stream, although really accurate humidiy control is difficult to achieve in practice due to variable solar radiation.

CARBON DIOXIDE ENRICHMENT
Recent years have brought considerable publicity to the enrichment of the greenhouse atmosphere with additional carbon dioxide, CO_2. This gas is of course present in the earth's atmosphere at the concentration of 300 parts per million. Under conditions of good light and high temperatures it has been found that the normal concentration of CO_2 may be a limiting factor to growth, which has resulted in the limitation of vegetative development and reduced quality of leaf and flower. Experimental work has been carried out with many crops, particularly lettuce and tomatoes (especially when young), as well as carnations and chrysanthemums, to name only a few. Enrichment of the greenhouse atmosphere can be achieved by burning propane or paraffin in a heating appliance, or in a special burner in the case of propane, and also by CO_2 in gaseous form (called liquid CO_2). 'Dry ice' can also be used. The problem is ensuring that over-enrichment does not occur, the desirable figure being in the order of 900 parts per million, but measurement of this is only possible by testing with special equipment, perhaps only a good investment on a commercial scale.

The use of straw bales for tomato growing results in atmospheric enrichment with CO_2, and even the application of farmyard manure gives an increase in CO_2. While undoubtedly CO_2 enrichment will become as popular in amateur circles as it is in commercial units, it is important to appreciate that to gain maximum benefit from CO_2 enrichment, a fair degree of precision is necessary, otherwise the practice is merely wasteful. A considerable amount of technical data is presently available on the whole technique, and can be obtained from the manufacturers of technical equipment, fuel suppliers, and of course advisory services.

9 Essential equipment

BENCHING AND SHELVES FOR GREENHOUSES

Slatted wood open type benches are constructed with 4 in. $\times$ $\frac{3}{4}$ in. pressure treated wood fitted into either angle iron or patent galvanised angle steel fitments. Solid benches can also be readily made with galvanised corrugated iron or asbestos used instead of wood. Alternatively benches can be made entirely of wood. For convenience benches should be of table height, i.e. 30–34 in., and around 3 to $3\frac{1}{2}$ ft. wide to permit ease of working. Single level slatted benches are ideal for pot plants and boxes of seedlings, also for those aspects of propagation which depend on boxes or pots, as the warm air can readily pass through the benches. Solid benching is more desirable for filling with rooting mediums for cuttings, and of course for mist bench propagation units (see page 60). Some gardeners feel that solid benches should also be used exclusively for pot plants, to reduce watering needs, and there is some virtue in this philosophy, especially as capillary watering can then be readily achieved (see page 58). Where solid benches are used, it is *essential* to allow an air space between the outside of the greenhouse and the bench to permit the passage of warm air between the bench and the outside of the greenhouse. Shelves at high level are often favoured by gardeners, especially for keeping plants near the light during the winter months. Two or more tiered benches can also be used, the lower levels being ideal for overwintering dahlia tubers or chrysanthemum stools. Much in fact can be achieved by the imaginative gardener in the whole realm of benching to make the best use of available greenhouse space.

WATERING AND FEEDING EQUIPMENT
The application of water to greenhouse crops or plants can be as simple as a watering can and a supply of water from a tap. In recent years, however, there has been an almost complete conversion to fully or semi-automatic watering and feeding systems in commercial circles. These are largely based on either overhead or low level spray lines, trickle nozzle systems, 'lay flat' polythene, or individual tube systems for pot plants. Virtually all systems can be operated through electronic equipment which phases the application of the water and, if necessary, soluble nutrients, when dilutors are used. Such equipment is now becoming available to the amateur gardener and full information can be obtained from the specialist firms involved in greenhouse irrigation.

Varying degrees of sophistication are possible with all watering and liquid nutrient supplying apparatus. The first stage in the latter is perhaps a bottle dilutor for installing between the tap and the hose pipe outlet, allowing liquid nutrients to be given simultaneously with water at the desired dilution.

Spraylines which supply water in fine mist form can also be fairly easily fitted in a small greenhouse, provided there is adequate pressure and volume of water (40–60 p.s.i), and bottle dilutors can also be incorporated in such equipment. Solenoid valves are relatively inexpensive pieces of equipment, these being electrically controlled valves which will allow water to be applied through any system of irrigation at the turn of a switch. Ceramic blocks control water application on the basis of evaporation from an absorbent surface.

Watering cans for greenhouses are available in metal or plastic and they should preferably have long spouts and fine rose.

CAPILLARY BENCHES

Capillary watering systems are becoming very popular, especially for pot plant growers. Here a completely level bench is lined with polythene to give an absolutely tight basin some 3 to 4 inches in depth. A perforated pipe is led down the centre of the bench, preferably inside some small diameter drainage tiles or sections of curved asbestos, to avoid blockage of holes in pipe. Rough gritty sand of acceptable capillarity is then put in the basin to give about a 4-in. layer. By the use of a fish tank and a ball cock, a controlled water level can readily be maintained about $\frac{1}{2}$ to 1 in. below the top of the sand. A capillary bench can also be operated with drip nozzles or even a slow running hose. Pot plants are then spaced out on top of the bench and will absorb water by capillary pull. Nutrients can be introduced to the bench also, taking care not to use these at too strong a dilution. Plastic pots are more effective than clay pots with this system. Modifications of this system can also be used for ring culture of tomatoes and other crops. An electronic controller can be used to control water application.

SOIL AND BENCH WARMING

Soil or bench warming involves the use of electrical cables to warm the actual growing or propagating medium, or impart warmth to it in various receptacles. There is, first of all, the use of 12 gauge wire (of known electrical resistance), and this is used in conjunction with transformers to give a safe low voltage (6–30 volts). This system is more popular for the warming of borders intended for crops, or for cold frames. The 12 gauge wire should be laid at a depth of 9 to 10 in. and at 3 to 9 in. apart, depending on loading, which will lie between 5 and 10 watts per sq. ft.

Mains voltage cables can also be used, in the same general way but these can be dangerous if cultivation is practiced when the system is in operation, and they are therefore better for propagating benches. Benches can, however, be warmed by either the low or mains voltage system, especially when mist propagation is being carried out, the loading in this instance being higher, around 15 watts per sq. ft., to permit the necessary high temperature (75°F.) for this technique.

CONTROL OF SOIL AND BENCH WARMING

The control of electricity input to soil warming installations can take three forms. The dosage method is where the heating is put in operation for a fixed period each day or night, generally at off-peak tariff times. While the temperature of the border or bench will fall during the period when the heating is not in operation, the drop is not significant. Time clock operation can be employed, although generally speaking 8 to 10 hours of operation in each 24 is sufficient.

The second method is by the use of a thermostat embedded horizontally in the actual media, this being the best method for all forms of propagation installations where higher temperatures are constantly desirable.

The third method is by inspection, where by the use of a soil thermometer, checks are kept on the temperature of the medium and the requisite dosage of electricity applied.

The basic principles involved in the use of soil and bench warming techniques are two-fold. First there is the fact that many plants will grow satisfactorily in lower air temperatures, provided the growing medium is warm. Thus the growing medium can be kept warm by reasonably economic means, allowing lower greenhouse air temperatures to prevail. This is particularly true also of the pre-warming period prior to planting a heat-loving crop such as tomatoes, it being possible to bring the growing medium up to the required temperature in a very short time, instead of the lengthy period required where growing mediums are warmed by convection currents from the conventional heating system and pipes filled with hot water are nowhere in contact with the soil.

The second important facet of soil warming is associated with the same principle, but more precisely. Where limited amounts of propagating medium are desired at high temperatures to assist rapid rooting, electrical soil warming really comes into its own.

There is no need to grope for information on the subject of soil or bench warming, or for that matter on the whole realm of electrical power usage, as technical advice is readily available from electricity boards and from suppliers of equipment.

PROPAGATION CASES AND MIST PROPAGATION UNITS

The vegetative production of new plants from sections depends entirely on inducing the formation of sufficient root development to make the tissue self supporting as quickly as possible. The problem is to maintain the vegetative tissue in good condition so that healthy root formation can take place, a situation unlikely where soft leaf tissue is involved and wilting takes place. Propagation cases are based on the principle that by raising the temperature and humidity so that the atmosphere is charged with moisture, the normal moisture loss through the leaves by transpiration is reduced to the minimum, thus maintaining the turgidity of the vegetative tissue and ensuring that it is in good condition for producing new roots.

The term 'propagating case' refers, in the accurate sense, to a conveniently sized cold frame sash set up either over a box or on a propagating bench, with some system of bottom heat to ensure the constantly warm conditions required. The temperature and humidity within the propagating case can be maintained independently of the temperature and humidity of the greenhouse, indeed this is why it is a most useful propagating tool. A polythene bag over a box or pot emulates the same principle, as indeed does a sheet of glass over a deep box or plastic propagators for seed trays. Propagating cases can of course be bought complete, some with supplementary and others with full lighting, so that they are, in effect, growth rooms.

MIST PROPAGATION

Mist propagation was developed to avoid the drawbacks of the propagating case, which largely centres around the heat which can be developed within the case, as this can be detrimental to plants. A soil warmed bench is maintained at a temperature of 70–75° F. (see page 58) and is used in conjunction with a series of vertical mist nozzles placed approx. 4 ft. apart and 2 ft. high (according to pressure of water and purpose). The object is to maintain a film of moisture over the propagating material, so that by the elementary principle of loss of heat by evaporation, the propagating material is kept cool and transpiration is kept to the minimum, thus inducing rapid rooting, provided there is sufficient warmth in the propagating medium. This must be free-draining to avoid saturation, coarse inert sand being ideal.

The film of moisture is maintained and saturation of the rooting medium avoided by a sensing device known as an electronic 'leaf' which switches on and off the supply of water to the mist nozzles. It is important to ensure that the correct type of leaf is obtained for the type of water inherent to the area, it having been found that with very pure water supplies, such as that of the Glasgow area for example, one form of leaf will not operate satisfactorily, there being insufficient salt in the water to close the circuit. Water pressure to operate the mist nozzles must be sufficiently high, 45 to 60 lbs. per sq. in., and if this is not available from the mains supply, pressurised tanks will be needed. (Full details of mist nozzle equipment are available from irrigation equipment suppliers.)

WEANING
This is the process whereby plants are gradually returned to normal greenhouse conditions. It is achieved by gradually reducing the number of mist applications and reducing the root temperature. While this can be carried out manually, weaning units are available which will do the task automatically by setting the control gear accordingly.

10 Illumination

There are four quite separate issues to be considered here. The first is the simple one of providing lighting for working convenience, this being readily achieved with waterproof light fittings. Make sure that the light bulbs are positioned correctly so that the light is directed to the best advantage to avoid undue shadow, especially if a particular bench or corner is frequently worked at during the hours of darkness or during dull weather.

EXTENDED LIGHTING FOR MANIPULATION OF DAY LENGTH

This makes use of low intensity light in the order of 5 to 10 watts per sq. ft. and is of great value for bringing forward delaying or increasing the flowering performance of photoperiodic plants such as mid and late flowering chrysanthemums, carnations, pelargoniums, and a whole lot of subjects. One would require to study the basic principles and actual techniques of extended lighting in some detail before attempting to apply it practically, and some reference will be made, where applicable, when consideration is given to specific crops.

It will suffice, at this stage, to say that many plants respond to the duration of light as well as to its intensity, and indeed their growth is controlled according to the season of the year and the length of daylight appropriate to it. Mid and late season chrysanthemums develop vegetatively until the daylight is less than around $14\frac{1}{2}$ hours, generally around mid-September, when flower buds are then induced by virtue of the impulse given by the shorter period of light. By a process of shading when the daylight hours are longer than $14\frac{1}{2}$, or by a period of extended light, generally by 60 watt Tungsten filament lights at 4 ft. spacings, or 100 watt at 6 ft. spacings, applied for a duration according to season of between 2 and 5 hours in the middle of the night on the 'cyclic' technique (3 minutes on and 9 minutes off), responsive chrysanthemums can be induced to grow regularly and flower at almost any time of the year, although the quality of bloom will deteriorate in poor light areas during the winter months, due to the lower total light intensity, which of course is still necessary for photosynthesis purposes.

Pot plants such as pelargoniums can respond to short periods of low intensity light in the middle of the night by being much more floriferous, for reasons which are still not fully understood.

Dahlia tubers can be induced to produce more cuttings by the same basic methods, but in this case high intensity light is needed.

SUPPLEMENTARY LIGHTING

The third use of lights is where natural daylight is supplemented by artificial light of a sufficiently high intensity to stimulate rapid photosynthesis. This is of value when raising light demanding plants such as tomatoes or cucumbers during the early spring when natural light may be of a low order.

The best fitments to use are those known as high power mercury vapour lights, each of which will cost in the order of £20, to illuminate an area of 4 ft. × 3ft. 6in. It is therefore only of value for young plants for a limited period, generally 2 to 3 weeks immediately after pricking off tomatoes or cucumbers, for a period of up to 16 hours per day. 200 watt mercury vapour lamps with built-in reflectors are also available at a much lower price and will illuminate 4 sq. ft. More specific information should be obtained beforehand.

GROWING ROOMS

The last use of light is where artificial light completely replaces natural light in a building of high thermal insulation. This is now being carried out commercially by bedding plant producers and also by tomato growers. In all cases, propagation time is much reduced, especially as with bedding plants continuous lighting can be given. Growing rooms require to be properly constructed, with fan circulation to control temperature, and, if necessary, staged heaters to maintain temperatures at an acceptable level. Associated equipment involves a dark germinating cabinet where seeds are germinated at 95–100% humidity.

The cost of such sophisticated equipment is presently at a level which is unlikely to attract amateur gardeners, although looking a few years into the future it seems likely that basements or old brick garages will be serving as 'greenhouses' for a wide range of activities. Some firms are, however, now offering small portable 'growing rooms' at attractive prices, in addition to small propagating cases with supplementary lights to help plants over a poor light period.

Important note: The rapid progress being made in the whole realm of artificial lighting for plant growth necessitates constant re-appraisal of existing techniques, as more information flows in all the time. Such information is available from the Electricity Council or through the appropriate technical adviser with the various Electricity Boards, in addition to official advisory services, and gardeners would be well advised to seek such authoritative and up to date information before becoming too deeply involved in any particular sphere.

11 The basic rules of greenhouse gardening

A green plant has a root, a stem, leaves and ultimately in most cases a flower, followed by a fruit or seed, and it will, if given suitable growing conditions, adhere to a fairly regular pattern of growth. The native habitat of many of the plants we grow is often vastly different, climatically speaking, to that prevailing in Britain, and a greenhouse is merely a device for overcoming climatic disadvantages. Modern breeding, however, has very much altered the basic characteristics of many plants, simply because nature's own handiwork may not suit the demanding horticulturist in respect of flowering or fruiting habits. The plant breeder has endeavoured to blend all the best qualities of many different varieties and groups of plants to ensure optimum quality and performance, not always entirely successfully, but generally with a fair measure of success, as can be seen when one looks at the wonderful modern range of all the different plants and crops we grow, not only in our greenhouse, but out of doors as well.

**'Blue Chips', an
attractive double gloxinia**

The best time to start gloxinia
tubers is in February or March

The really important thing to appreciate about greenhouse gardening is that while nothing is vastly altered in the whole cycle of growth from seed or cutting to mature plant, we are dealing, in many cases, with groups of plants whose natural habitat is far away, and this makes them just that bit different from the plants which are true natives. There is more to this philosophy than mere tenderness and lack of ability to stand up to frost. Tomatoes came from sunny South America originally and still, despite intense breeding, yearn for all the light they can get, especially in their early days when we try to induce them to grow in our dreary winter. Many plants are natives of the Equatorial forests and long for the hot humid shady conditions typical of these regions. There are also lots of perfectly hardy plants which are not always grown out of doors because we wish to extend or alter their season of production, lettuce being a good example of this.

The really vital thing to appreciate with all greenhouse gardening is that a largely artificial growing regime is being created merely for our own convenience. There is light and air, but little or no moisture unless we supply it. The sun often shines to excess in summer and steps have to be taken in expel the trapped heat. Plants grow much more quickly in a greenhouse than they do out of doors, so that more moisture and nutrients are needed to sustain this rapid growth.

DAY AND NIGHT TEMPERATURE DIFFERENCE

Another highly important issue with all plants in a greenhouse is the differing conditions between day and night, especially during spring or autumn when sunny days are often followed by cold nights. The result is a tremendous temperature variation which can give rise to unbalanced growth.

A gardener, to a certain extent, creates an exclusive growing environment in his greenhouse which is different from that in other greenhouses, and certainly very different from that in the garden. This is especially the case where pot plant growing and ring culture of tomatoes and other plants are concerned, involving limited quantities of growing medium which can, at the outset, be pest and disease free and in a certain physical and nutrient state, more or less under the control of the gardener. This is a tremendous advantage as results are much more predictable than they are out of doors. This facet should be fully exploited and no chances taken with doubtful materials, particularly with reference to the various propagating mediums, seed sowing and potting composts used for various crops.

ESSENTIAL ELEMENTS FOR PLANT GROWTH

All green plants are dependent on the supply of essential air, moisture, and simple elements to allow them to carry on the manufacturing process which takes place in the green leaves and is vital to sustain development right up to the ultimate production of flowers, fruits or 'seeds'. The elements, which are often called nutrients, are mostly taken up in soluble form via the root system of the plant and thereafter transported to where they are most urgently required. The range of these elements is similar, whether for outside or inside growth, in large or small batches of soil.

The first essentials for a growing plant or germinating seed may well merely be moisture, air and a suitable temperature to trigger off growth or induce a cutting to form roots, when thereafter demand for everything increases according to the size of plant, time of year, nature of the plant and other variable factors. Nutrients are present in nearly all growing mediums and their presence can be supplemented either by applying organic or inorganic fertilisers in powdered or liquid form. Plants, of course, can readily absorb soluble nutrients through their leaves and stems, and this has resulted recently in great interest in foliar feeding.

To gloss over the importance of plant nutrition would be foolish, yet it would be equally silly to delve too deeply into a subject which would merit a whole series of books, let alone a few paragraphs. Apart from the notes which follow, it is, I feel, much better to deal in more detail with the practical problems of plant nutrition under the respective notes which I will give on growing mediums and culture.

Fertilizers and liquid feeds are available in bewildering array and must always be used according to directions. It is worth noting that many plants respond equally well to foliar feeding as opposed to the application of nutrients to the soil.

12 Nutritional aspects of greenhouse culture

Any discussion on plant nutrients should, I feel, always be prefaced by the warning that it is wrong to think of plant nutrition in a compartmentalised manner, as there is necessarily an intimate co-relationship between the range of nutrients which go to make up the complete plant diet. The diet of a baby will not be that of an adult, and the same is true of plants. Nor is exactly the same diet necessary or required by different plants. The really important issue of plant nutrition is the balance of nutrients in relation to each other. As plants in a greenhouse grow quicker than they do out of doors, and in many instances are grown in limited amounts of soil, it is important to maintain a balanced nutrient level throughout the whole growing period of the plant, until perhaps in time the limited amount of growing medium is physically played out and requires renewal.

LIME AND ALKALINITY
The sweetness or sourness of any individual constituent or complete growing medium is measured by what is known as a pH scale, which gives an accurate indication of the calcium content (see page 70). The ideal pH figure varies according to the species of plant to be grown, but generally speaking all plants require lime, except those which are unable to tolerate it in large amounts; furthermore, calcium helps to keep the growing media sweet by neutralising the acid excretion of micro-organisms and is therefore essential for plant nutrition, especially where there is great dependence on chemical change. Recent findings on the growing of plants in all-peat or peat/sand composts (see page 83) have, however, shown that a much lower pH figure can be tolerated. The reasons for this are somewhat obscure, but they centre around the initially sterile nature of these composts and the straight absorption of their nutrient content at the outset, uncomplicated by micro-organism activity.

THE MAIN OR MACRO ELEMENTS
Nitrogen
While nitrogen can be added to composts in several forms, the growing plant eventually takes it up as nitrate. The role of nitrogen is generally stated as being concerned largely with leaf development, and this no doubt is theoretically the case. An excess of nitrogen in relation to the other elements, especially potash, can result in gross fleshy growth, to the detriment of flowers and fruit, with the reverse being the case when there is a shortage of nitrogen. Colour of leaf, too, is often a fair measure of the availability or otherwise of nitrogen, a very dark green denoting excess, sickly pale green denoting deficiency.

Potassium (K_2O)
The role of potash is a complex one, it being intrinsically involved with photosynthesis and the formation of fruit and seed, and it certainly has a vital role to play in colour pigmentation. An excess of potash can result in extremely hard dark growth, whereas shortage (or unavailability) has the reverse effect. There is a vital correlationship between nitrogen and potassium, and the growing of many crops such as tomatoes depends largely on the correct manipulation of the availability of these two elements.

Phosphorus (P_2O_5)
Applied in various forms, phosphorus is taken up by the plant as phosphoric acid, following a somewhat complicated exchange mechanism in the soil, it being necessary for the soil to be fairly sweet before the phosphorus is available. Phosphorus has a number of duties to perform in plant physiology – assisting good root development, early maturing, and many other issues. An excess or shortage of phosphorus is difficult to pinpoint visually, a dark green or bluish colour being the best yardstick to its unavailability.

Magnesium
Now considered of much more importance than hitherto, magnesium is generally concerned with the vital process of photosynthesis or food manufacture in the leaves of the

green plant. Some crops make large demands on this element, including tomatoes. The availability of magnesium to the plant would appear to be very largely tied up with the available levels of potash, and for most cultural practices magnesium should be present in adequate amounts. Deficiency symptoms are shown by an interveinal chlorosis or lightening of the leaf colour, followed by a bronze colouration. Excess of magnesium is seldom a problem.

THE OTHER OR MICRO ELEMENTS
Iron
This is an important element, frequently rendered unavailable in alkaline soils or when excess lime is applied. The deficiency of iron is possibly the easiest of all to recognise, leaves becoming extremely yellow or even white. Frequent problems can arise with iron deficiency, especially with pot plants such as Hydrangeas or Primulas, although nowadays the use of sequestrated compounds has done much to overcome this.

Manganese
Does not generally give cause for concern, except for a crop such as tomatoes growing in an acid soil, following steam sterilisation, the plant becoming extremely brittle and almost blueish in colour and caused by an excess of manganese. This is a matter for specialist advice.

Sulphur
This is needed by all plants, but only in infinitesimal amounts.

Boron
Should rarely cause concern for greenhouse culture, boron excess or deficiency largely being a problem of brassicas out of doors. Boron deficiency has recently caused some concern with tomatoes, causing leaf scorch and fruit bronzing. Molybdenum, selenium, sodium and a few other elements all go to make up the complete diet, but all of these should be available if balanced fertilisers and manures are used.

13 Soil analysis

Finding out the nutrient level of soils, with particular emphasis on the calcium content, is frequently of great concern to the greenhouse gardener. The simplest and best way of dealing with this matter is to have soils, or specific ingredients for formulating growing media, analysed in a laboratory. There are few areas in Britain where this service is not available.

Alternatively soil analysis kits can be used, following the directions supplied with them. Unfortunately, however, soil analysis kits have their limitations, although they are extremely useful for quick checks, as laboratory analysis can take time.

LABORATORY ANALYSIS
Information is generally given on various aspects:

Organic matter. This shows the level of organic matter within the soil and states whether this is low, medium or high. It is sometimes given only if specifically requested.

Calcium. The information given centres around pH and lime requirement. The pH scale is from 1 to 14 but only figures in the 5 to 8 range are likely to interest the gardener. The figure 7 is neutral, and for most plants a figure between 6 and 7 is desirable for soil based composts, a figure of between 5 and 6 apparently being acceptable for soil-less mediums. It is important to remember that when soils are laboratory analysed, the lime requirement to achieve a specific pH figure is *given* in amounts of lime (generally ground limestone) to apply per sq. yd. To convert this to bushels, it is estimated that in a square yard of soil to digging depth there are approximately 5 bushels (22 × 10 × 12 in.). Hydrated lime is frequently used for application to greenhouse borders, although it is not advised for composts as it is a little 'hot', ground limestone being better. Less hydrated lime is required per sq. yd., only approximately three quarters of the amount stated for ground limestone. Calcium carbonate or chalk is a soft form of lime and has the same liming value as ground limestone, which tends to be too coarse particled for composts. It should be noted that soil testing kits do not provide an actual lime requirement, merely a pH figure, the application of lime being calculated to a rough formula.

Available nitrogen (N). Some laboratories may carry out this test, while others do not. Although it is a useful figure for 'spot check' work during the growing season, the nitrogen level varies tremendously according to the time of year, age of compost, whether steam sterilised or not, and a whole host of other factors. Where a nitrogen level is given it will merely state whether the soil is high, medium or low in this element or a figure will be given in parts per million (p.p.m.) or mgms. per 100 gms.

Available potassium (K$_2$0). The level of this is stated as high, medium or low and also sometimes in p.p.m. and mgms. per 100 gms., and these terms are a useful guide to the fertility of the soil in respect of potassium content.

Available phosphorus (P$_2$0$_5$). Here again the level is given as high, medium or low, and figures in p.p.m. and mgms. per 100 gms. may also be available, in respect of the so-called available phosphorus. This information can be a useful guide, but one upon which too much reliance should not be placed, as much of the phosphoric acid can become 'fixed' in the soil, some soils which have been used for years showing an abnormally high level of phosphorus.

Soluble salt content. This is a figure given by the laboratory analyst as pC or C F, and is one of the most useful facets of laboratory analysis, as it shows the quantities of fertiliser, or their bases, in solution in the soil. Plants are particularly sensitive, in varying degrees, to the soluble salt content of the growing medium, because they derive their water supply by the process of osmosis which depends on the ability of the higher concentration of salt in the cell of the plant to draw in water through the cell wall. Soluble nutrients move in along with the water, by absorption. If, however, the salt content in the soil is higher than that of the plant, the process can be reversed or slowed down, according to varying concentrations. Over-application of fertiliser to the soil will bring about this state of affairs, showing the need for selecting the correct compost for a particular type of plant, and the care necessary to avoid an excess of fertiliser application.

SPECTROGRAPHIC ANALYSIS
In special instances spectrographic analysis can be carried out to determine the level of the other elements in the soil, but this is a technique only merited for instances where abnormal growth is evident and it is generally deemed necessary only by an advisory officer or consultant.

TISSUE ANALYSIS
There is increasing popularity in the analysis of plant tissue, by spectrographic or other means, to find out the respective levels of nutrients present in this. Here again this is a technique which would require the blessing of an advisory officer or consultant, and it is generally reserved for finding out the reason for abnormalities, although the use of tissue analysis for spot checks is increasing, especially in the U.S.A.

ALGAE OBSERVATION
A more recent technique involves the observation of various algae which are introduced on to the soil sample and grown under laboratory conditions.

VISUAL OBSERVATION
Despite all forms of analysis, laboratory or otherwise, much more importance is now being placed on visual assessment of growth, which in a way is ironical, as this surely is what intuitive gardeners have been doing for years.

14 Soil sterilisation

The term 'sterilisation' is an unfortunate one, as it indicates that a completely sterile medium is involved. With soil this is neither necessary nor advisable. 'Pasteurisation' is a happier word, as this indicates that merely the harmful organisms are killed off, leaving behind the beneficial ones, this applying particularly to the nitrifying bacteria.

Soil sterilisation can be carried out in a variety of ways, some of which are unfortunately not convenient or practical for the amateur gardener.

STEAM STERILISATION
There are two forms of steam sterilisation. The first involves the use of perforated pipes through which pressurised steam is led into the soil. It is necessary to allow a period of 20 to 25 minutes to allow the top 10 to 12 in. of soil to reach at least 180°F. (Generally 200°F.). A P.V.C. sheet is placed on top of the soil and allowed to remain in position for some time after the steam is shut off, to retain the heat.

Low pressure steam sterilisation can be carried out in a variety of ways, all centring round the boiling of water below the soil, which is held on a perforated steel plate or in small sacks. Low pressure steam sterilisers can be built to the John Innes specification or constructed to any convenient design (Fig. 7). Normally a 10–12 in. layer of soil is placed loosely in position above the boiling water. This is a much slower method than pressurised steam and takes 2 to 3 hours or more, according to soil type, for the top layer of soil to achieve the necessary 180°F.

More recent methods of steam sterilisation in commercial circles involve the leading of steam in under large P.V.C. sheets, this being called *sheet steaming*. The heat passes downwards through the soil by progressive heat exchange as the steam condenses on the soil surface. Research work is now aiming to reduce the sterilisation temperature, possibly to between 160° and 180°F., by cooling the steam with air, in an effort to reduce the toxic effects which can result when soil is over-sterilised (see also page 75). Nevertheless, virus disease would not seem to be destroyed at temperatures under 180–190°F. so it is doubtful whether this modified method will have much application for areas known to be virus infected.

OTHER METHODS OF HEAT STERILISATION
Various methods are now practiced, using both naked flame and dry heat. The naked flame methods rely largely on a revolving drum placed horizontally in such a way that soil circulated within the drum drops through a flame and progresses from one end, out of the other. These units are obviously too large and expensive to be of much interest to the amateur however, and their efficiency varies due to condition of soil.

An alternative involves the soil being sterilised on a vibrating plate, again a method for the professional.

Possibly the best method of dry heat sterilisation on a small scale is the use of electric sterilisers, which are available in various sizes. Other methods of 'dry' heat sterilisation merely rely on wet soil being held on a metal plate beneath which a fire is built. In all cases involving dry heat or open flames, the effectiveness of sterilisation depends on the period of time the soil is subjected to the heat. With well-designed equipment this has been taken into account and soil is properly pasteurised. Home-made equipment, however, suffers from the drawback of being merely as efficient as the operator, the heat method over an open fire frequently resulting in the soil being baked, which not only renders it sterile but also burns up the organic matter, thus destroying soil texture.

HOT WATER STERILISATION
For many years thought to be extremely suspect, hot water sterilisation is now coming back into vogue. Boiling water is applied to shallow layers of soil which are covered with *clean* sacks to retain the heat as long as possible.

Note: While the effectiveness of all methods of heat sterilisation can be judged on the cropping results obtained, a good sensitive *soil* thermometer in a non-conducting sheath can do much to ensure that the temperature reached during the actual sterilisation process is of an acceptable level, 160–180°F. being the norm.

CHEMICAL STERILISATION

A range of chemicals is available for soil sterilisation, some of which are not available or advisable for amateur use in view of the difficulties of application and the toxicity factor of the chemicals involved. The powdered form of Metham Sodium (Basamid) is, however, available for amateur use, and is extremely simple to work with and highly effective. Liquid forms of Metham Sodium are widely used in professional circles and have a slightly different action on the soil. Basically speaking, following application a gas is released which is effective in dealing with a wide range of soil borne maladies. Either borders or heaps of soil can be treated, *in both cases following directions to the letter.* It should be noted that severe damage will ensue to plants receiving any fumes during application and for up to 40 days afterwards (depending on temperature).

The only other chemicals I would recommend for amateur use are Formaldehyde, Dithane and Cresylic Acid. Formaldehyde is applied at a dilution of 1:49 at 5 gallons per sq. yd., the soil being covered with sacks, and this chemical is largely effective against common root rots. Dithane is now used for the same purpose. Cresylic Acid is also reasonably effective and is highly effective against pests. It is used in a similar manner to Formaldehyde.

Special Note: Sterilised soil is *not* immunised and can often be more readily recontaminated with pests and diseases than unsterilised soil.

MATERIAL	Root Eelworm	Root Rots	Vert. Wilt	Virus (TMV) Mosaic	Damping off Disease	Weeds	Treatment to planting (days)
STEAM (including properly applied dry heat & hot water) (180°F)	C	C	C	C (good at 194°F)	C	C	7–14
Metham Sodium (Results variable)	C	C	P	X	C	C	40
Formaldehyde	X	P	P (good at 60°F)	X	P	X	20–40
Dithane	X	P	X	X	P	X	3–14
Cresylic acid	P	X	P	X	P	X	18–20
D.D. (by injection)	C	X	X	X	X	X	40
Carbon Bi-sulphide (by injection)	C	X	X	X	X	X	7
* Methyl Bromide	C	C	P	X	C	C	4
* Chloropicrin	X	C	C	X	C	X	20

ABBREVIATIONS C = Control
P = Partial control
X = No control
* Not available to amateurs

15 Cold and heated frames

ACCLIMATISATION AND HARDENING OFF
A frame is a piece of equipment which is complementary to a greenhouse, especially where greenhouse raised plants are to be allowed to grow for a period out of doors. The real virtue of a frame lies in its ability to acclimatise greenhouse raised plants to outside conditions, this being achieved by progressive ventilation, at first only for a limited period during good bright days only, progressively increasing this during good days, until the final stage is reached, when the frame sashes are removed during the day only to begin with and then left off completely day and night.

OTHER USES OF FRAMES
Frames can of course be used for the culture of crops, propagation and a whole host of other activities. Indeed frame culture is a subject on its own and one which would, in fact, require a specialised book. Many of the basic principles of greenhouse culture described in this book will, of course, apply to frame culture also.

TYPES OF FRAMES
The 6 × 4 ft. English sash, composed of small panes of glass and weighing a great deal, is set on a brick base, but this type is a thing of the past in the amateur garden. In its place has come the Dutch Light frame, composed of a single sheet of glass and measuring approx. 5 ft. × 2½ ft., also steel framed sashes in a range of forms, all of which are light and easy to handle. The Dutch Light sash can either be set up on concrete blocks or on a brick base wall. Alternatively foundations can be made of wood. It is advisable to have a rear height of 12 to 14 in. and a front height of 9 to 10 in., this giving a sufficient fall. Cold frames are generally sited running from east to west, with the slope of the frame facing south to catch all available light, unless of course they are required for shade loving subjects exclusively, or for propagation, when the frame can be facing north or placed in a shady position. Frames can also be double span. Frames can readily be

linked on to the base wall of a greenhouse, this being common years ago, and it is still sound practice today for economical heating.

HEATING OF FRAMES
While it may be convenient to link greenhouse heating to the frame, especially if the system is the small bore type, it is more usual to depend on soil warming. This can be carried out in much the same way as described for propagating benches, either with low or mains voltage cables, at a loading of $7\frac{1}{2}$ watts per sq. ft.

Soil warming cables may of course also be placed in the actual soil of the frames, at a depth of 8–9 in. (below shallow cultivation level) for the growing of early lettuce and other crops such as strawberries.

Mineral Insulated cables, set along the side of the frame, in porcelain holders are most convenient for frost protection.

CONSTRUCTION OF FRAMES
Factory made frames are merely set up according to directions, while other types have the ground assembly built to suit the size of sash. Cement blocks are becoming extremely popular for frame ground work. If using wooden base 'walls' ensure that the wood is pressure treated with preservative. Polythene (500 gauge) can be used with good effect in lieu of glass to make excellent lightweight frame sashes.

16 Composts and growing mediums

Horticulturally speaking, compost has two meanings, and this tends to give rise to some confusion. The controlled breakdown of organic matter such as grass cuttings, haulms of peas or beans, and garden refuse generally, produces a valuable source of so-called 'humus' which has an important role to play in gardening. The term 'compost' is also applied to growing mediums and refers to a formulated mixture of peat and sand, with or without soil, and in most cases supplied with plant nutrients to enable a wide range of crops and plants to be grown for varying periods in pots or containers. Materials other than peat, sand and soil, some of which are synthetic, can also be used as growing mediums. Recent years have seen much work being carried out on the use of growing mediums entirely divorced from 'normal' organic matter, such as waste paper, and time will perhaps see the word 'compost' having a more singular meaning.

There has been much research over many years to try and evolve the ideal growing medium to suit a wide range of crops and plants and thus avoid the complications of countless different formulae. The basic aim has always been for standardisation of composts in order that predictable results can be achieved. Unfortunately the creation of such a material is limited by the variability of the specific ingredients themselves, as these tend to differ considerably according to their precise nature and source of origin. Soil from one garden or field can have vastly different physical and nutritional qualities than soil from another, as indeed can sand and peat, and it would be unrealistic to pretend otherwise. One can be assured, however, that if a fairly broad set of rules is adhered to, results can be consistently good.

THE BASIC INGREDIENTS OF COMPOSTS
Loam. Ideally loam is the product of a 4–5 in. thick turf lifted from a grass pasture or well managed turf area and stacked grass downwards for a sufficiently long period to allow the grass plants and their roots to partially rot, six months or more being a suitable period. Obviously the nature of loam can vary enormously, according to soil classification in any particular area and how it has been managed over the years. Here indeed lies the weakness of trying to achieve standardisation, particularly as supplies of reliable loam are becoming increasingly difficult to obtain. Frequently

'soil' from the top 9–12 in. is used as a substitute for loam, but this generally has a lower organic matter content, coupled with which the mineral content may vary from large particled sand to fine particled sticky clay or silt. Add to these variables the still further complication of nutrient level, acidity or sweetness, the possible presence of weeds, pests and diseases, especially potato root eelworm cysts, and it can be seen why loam or soil is such an unknown factor. Loam or soil should, of course, always be sterilised before use (see Chapter 14).

Peat. Many different types of peat are available in Britain and elsewhere, variability being due to derivation, age and depth of harvesting. The ideal peat for *composts* is cellular in texture and generally light in colour. Fine, 'dirty' peats, or conversely those which have a black decomposed look, should be either avoided or used along with cellular peats to provide trace elements. Peats are classified according to the Von Post scale which relates to the colour of water exuded by moist peat under pressure, the darker the exudation, the more humic and therefore less desirable the peat.

Good quality peat in a compost ensures excellent moisture retention, acting as it does like a sponge, and capable of storing up water and nutrients. At the same time it helps to give excellent aeration. On a long-term basis it provides a valuable source of 'humus', the colloidal in-between stage of organic decomposition, which gums the small mineral particles of soil together into a large composite structure ideal for micro-organic activity and chemical change. Peat is relatively inert and contains few quickly available plant nutrients. A good sample can be depended upon to contain neither pests, diseases nor weeds, thus making sterilisation unnecessary. The pH is generally in the region of 3.5 to 4. The present mode of distributing peat in polythene bags generally ensures that it is received in first class condition, not too dry and therefore ready for use.

Leaf mould. At one time this was extensively used as an ingredient of composts, yet it now seems to have fallen from favour, no doubt because it can, like loam, be an unknown quantity. Nevertheless, the excellent physical attributes of well-matured leaf mould from a mixed deciduous wooded

**Hyancinths for indoor display
potted in bulb fibre**

Impatiens (Balsam)—the perennial
greenhouse species may be propagated
from seed sown in gentle heat

area have endeared it to many gardeners, especially those seeking long-term composts for crops such as tomatoes and chrysanthemums.

Sand. Many different grades of sand are available, the important issues being neutral pH inertness, lack of contamination and good texture.

Vermiculite or Perlite. These two materials, which are expanded Mica and volcanic ash respectively, are by no means new to the horticultural scene. They are sterile, relatively inert and extremely light, yet at the same time able to absorb large quantities of moisture.

THE JOHN INNES COMPOSTS
These enjoy a worldwide reputation and were originally devised by Messrs. W. J. C. Lawrence and W. J. Newall of the John Innes Horticultural Institution.

John Innes Seed Compost (for seed sowing and very young plants, especially in winter)

2 parts (by bulk) of loam (preferably sterilised by heat)
1 part (by bulk) of peat
1 part (by bulk) of coarse sand

To each bushel (22 × 10 × 12in.) add $\frac{3}{4}$ oz. ground limestone and $1\frac{1}{2}$ oz. superphosphates.

John Innes Potting Compost

7 parts (by bulk) of loam
3 parts (by bulk) of peat
2 parts (by buik) of coarse sand

For the No. 1 compost add to each bushel $\frac{3}{4}$ oz. ground limestone, $\frac{1}{4}$ lb. John Innes Base Fertiliser (which is 2 parts by weight of hoof and horn meal, 2 parts superphosphates of lime, 1 part sulphate of potash).
For the No. 2 compost add $\frac{1}{2}$ lb. of the base fertiliser.
For the No. 3 compost add $\frac{3}{4}$ lb. of the base fertiliser.

The use of potting composts
John Innes Potting Compost No. 1 is best for young newly

pricked off seedlings, as if it is properly formulated it contains adequate nutrition to sustain the young plants for a short period, particularly if they are in large enough pots so that there is enough of the compost. The No. 2 mix could well damage or check young plants, having too high a pC. It is very much better to use John Innes No. 1 and apply liquid feeding as and when required. Generally speaking young plants should be fed as soon as they start to grow vigorously, but much will depend upon prevailing temperatures and whether the weather is bright or dull.

Apart from using J. I. composts for raising young plants up to the planting on stage, there is the further use of J. I. composts for full season growing, examples being ring culture or growing in limited quantities of growing medium, when the No. 2 compost is ideal. The use of No. 3 is risky, as it often has a pC (soluble salt) level which is too high for a young plant, and it should only be used for more mature plants such as chrysanthemums on their final potting.

THE U/C COMPOSTS

These are based on work carried out by the University of California and rely on sphagnum peat and fine sand, with nutrient additions. There are a great many different formulae, all of which can be bought ready formulated or with the necessary fertiliser to be added as required. It should be remembered that there is little reserve of nutrients in U/C composts and that where they are used, constant feeding with liquid nutrients is necessary. There is much to be said for the U/C composts as they can be readily mixed without the need for sterilisation, and avoid most of the complications of ammonia release which often follow when loams are sterilised. Popular U/C mixes are as follows:

For winter and early-spring use

Equal parts of peat moss and fine sand (by bulk)

add 2 oz. hoof and horn
$\frac{1}{5}$th oz. nitrate of potash
$\frac{1}{5}$th oz. sulphate of potash
2 oz. superphosphates
6 oz. magnesium limestone
2 oz. ground limestone

per bushel
(22 × 10 × 12 in.)
(after mixing
peat and sand)

For spring and summer use

Equal parts of peat moss and sand (by bulk)

add 4 oz. hoof and horn
 ¼ oz. ammonium nitrate   per bushel
 1 oz. sulphate of potash   (after mixing
 2 oz. superphosphates   peat and sand)
 4 oz. ground limestone
 2 oz. magnesium limestone

The hoof and horn meal should NOT be added until immediately before the compost is used.

 There are quite a few variations of the above theme and some gardeners prefer to add 5 to 8 oz. of ground limestone and a general fertiliser of a slow-acting type, particularly one containing trace elements. 75% peat and 25% sand is also preferred by some gardeners. 25% peat, and 75% sand can also be used. Coarser sands are more popular than fine sands.

Note: It is important to remember that plants grown in U/C composts have very little reserve of nutrients and will require feeding earlier and more frequently than those grown in a *good* John Innes compost, especially tomatoes.

U/C Composts for full-season growing

These composts can be used in containers for a full season crop, but feeding will be a constant process, otherwise there can be nutritional upsets.

ALL-PEAT COMPOSTS

These are available already formulated, both for seed sowing and the general growing of plants, and have proved to be very successful, especially for seed germination. Experience is needed with these composts if used as a full season growing medium, to enable best results to be obtained. Self-formulation should be along the lines of the U/C mixes, without sand but with the nutrient and lime additions.

OTHER COMPOSTS

Mixtures involving the use of leaf mould/soil, sand/soil, Vermiculite/peat, Perlite/peat, sand/farmyard manure, and a whole host of other formulae, can obviously only be talked about in general terms. Broadly speaking, however, those composts relying on materials containing few nutrients can be formulated along the lines of the U/C mixes, whereas with the other types some measure of the food value and pH of the ingredients would be necessary before they are used, or alternatively the results visually assessed. The only real test of any compost is the quality of the end product. In any case there has been, as stated earlier, a move away from variable composts to those of more or less standard composition, gardeners tending to use the compost which experience proves best.

COMPOST MIXING

All the ingredients for compost mixing should be under cover and reasonably dry. Mixing is best carried out on a cement floor, with the largest quantity (generally soil) placed on the floor first, followed by peat and sand. It is usual to turn all the ingredients several times before finally adding the accurately measured fertilisers to the final bulk, which should be applied separately, turning the one in before adding the others.

Important note: Always allow composts to warm up in the greenhouse before use.

17 Propagation

The word 'propagation' is perhaps rather high sounding. It means quite simply the raising of new plants by various means, and it is not necessarily a technique reserved exclusively for the greenhouse. Seed can be sown, cuttings inserted, and plants can be layered or grafted with fair dexterity out of doors, provided the subjects involved are hardy. With a greenhouse, however, especially if it is heated, propagation can be speeded up and the range of plant propagation can be considerably extended to include not only the hardy plants, many of which can be conveniently started in a greenhouse, but the whole galaxy of tender and half-hardy plants which must have some protection.

FACILITIES FOR PROPAGATION
The physical equipment for propagation has previously been alluded to (see page 60) and in general terms the object of all equipment or aids to propagation is to develop a self-supporting plant as quickly as possible.

MAIN MODES OF PROPAGATION
Basically there are two main forms of propagation, sexually by seed or asexually by vegetative means. From seed the first objective is to induce the breaking of the dormant period into which the embryo plant lapses when contained in a 'seed' of varying size and shape, and methods of achieving this vary. Propagation from seed can, of course, produce variable results, due to the cross pollination which may have occurred, although modern seed production methods can result in a remarkably 'true' seed formation, either where artificial means are adopted to prevent random cross pollination or where natural form or artificial breeding has resulted in flower formation which renders cross pollination botanically difficult or even impossible. Plant raising from seed is generally reasonably cheap. Certain types of plants can only be effectively propagated from seed, and this is also the only sure way of raising new varieties, apart from random or induced vegetative sporting.

Vegetative propagation, on the other hand, involves the production of roots on a portion of the plant's anatomy which can vary from stem, leaf, roots, corms, bulbs, to many other forms of plant tissue. The formation of roots can also vary from being simple to extremely difficult. In the majority of cases, vegetative propagation ensures an offspring with identical characteristics to the parent plant, and this method of propagation can be either rapid or the reverse, although it is generally the former.

With all types of propagation it is essential to start off with healthy seed or clean healthy vegetative portions of the plant. In the former case it generally means relying on a seedsman, or carefully self-saved seed, while in the latter case propagation material should only be selected from stock known to be healthy, especially as far as virus disease is concerned, otherwise infection is merely passed on to the new offspring. Elaborate precautions are taken by commercial establishments to keep stock healthy, this involving heat therapy in conditioning rooms, frequent inspection and roguing, and other methods. Much can also be done in respect of maintaining healthy plants by observing good hygiene – clean hands, knives, and containers, and by keeping a clean greenhouse. A good disinfectant for hands and tools is a useful item of greenhouse equipment.

THE REQUIREMENTS FOR PROPAGATION
These are quite simply air, moisture and a suitable temperature, whether seed or vegative propagation is involved. The exact requirements depend on species and are generally, but not always, associated with the inherent degree of hardiness. While the seeds of a hardy shrub such as berberis can be germinated out of doors, it might be much more convenient and quicker to germinate them in a warm greenhouse, and this is also true of a great number of hardy plants of various species. The same is true of cuttings or other vegetative sections of plants. There is no overall formula for success with propagation beyond attention to the general rules which have been found by experience to achieve the best results with any particular species.

SEED SOWING CONSIDERATIONS
When sowing any seed for greenhouse germination, the important considerations are as follows:

1 Size of seed
Some seeds are very tiny (e.g. lobelia, rhododendron), while others are large (e.g. sweet pea). The same seed compost, either John Innes, U/C, or all-peat mixes, are generally used

for all seeds, with modifications according to seed size, this applying to depth of sowing and degree of covering. Tiny seeds are best sown on the surface of the medium and merely pressed into the surface, or at the most covered with a layer of fine sand. Larger seeds are best covered to about the same depth as the size of the seed, or slightly more, and this is in fact a good general guide for all seeds.

2 Nature of seed

Some seeds have hard seed coats, and germination may be delayed because moisture cannot gain entry into the embryo until the seed coat rots or splits. While this will generally occur eventually, it is not always convenient to wait. Complementary to this is the breaking of the dormancy period into which seeds lapse, some for a considerable period. The two issues are not necessarily linked, as some seed with a hard seed coat may not be guilty of delayed germination, and all that may be required to soften the seed coat is immersion in hot water, thus allowing moisture to penetrate and trigger off the process of germination. Seeds known to be difficult to germinate, especially many shrubs and trees, are best subjected to the sort of treatment they receive in nature, which is generally alternate cold and warmth. Emulating this is not necessarily a greenhouse practice, as it merely consists of sowing the seed in receptacles and plunging them to their rims in the open garden. To finally encourage germination it may be necessary to eventually bring these seeds in their containers into a warm greenhouse. More recently refrigeration has been used to provide cold conditions for a few weeks, before bringing the seeds into the greenhouse. Some seeds, if sown immediately they are ripe, germinate without any trouble, whereas if they are allowed to lapse into dormancy, they can be difficult to germinate. This is the case with many of the alpines, primulas and ericas being notable in this respect.

CONTAINERS FOR SOWING

The quantity of seed involved has a large part to play in deciding upon a suitable container. Frequently clay or plastic seed 'pans' or bowls of varying dimensions are convenient for small batches. For large batches seed trays are used. These are available in wood, plastic and polystyrene. The standard size of seed tray is 14 × 9 × 2 in. (approx.). Fish boxes are, however, often used, but care should be taken to see that these are not contaminated with salt. The virtues and failings of the various containers can only be discovered by experience, although gardeners in recent years have placed great store on plastic seed trays, especially as there are few problems of sterilisation or deterioration, washing in warm water being sufficient in most instances, whereas wooden trays must be treated initially with preservative and regularly with formaldehyde if one is to be certain of freedom from disease. Plastic or polystyrene trays are excellent for capillary watering methods. Seed pans or bowls should also be carefully washed before use. More recently compartment-ised containers have come into use, both for seed sowing and pricking off, and these are certainly useful. Peat pots and soil blocks are also useful in this direction and can be packed in boxes. Plastic plant propagators can be used with plastic trays.

SOWING METHODS

Preparation of the containers for sowing can vary. Boxes generally only require a shallow layer of roughage such as rough peat or loam riddlings. Clay seed pans should have some broken pots/crocks placed over the drainage hole, and a little roughage, the latter only necessary for plastics. Compartmentised or individual containers are merely filled with compost. It is then seldom necessary to do more than fill the clean receptacle to its rim with the chosen seed compost (see Chapter 16) suitably warm and damp, ensuring even compaction, including the corners, and levelling off with a ruler. The compost is then pressed down with the base of another seed pan or piece of wood so that the surface is even. The compost can then be well watered and allowed to drain. Alternatively containers may be allowed to soak up water by standing them for a few minutes in a shallow tray containing an inch or so of water.

Seed is sown in a variety of ways. Fine seed is best scattered thinly on the surface and lightly pressed in, the con-tainer being held at eye level to ensure even sowing. Larger seeds are either scattered on and covered with some more compost rubbed through a fine riddle or perforated zinc at *low* level (e.g. $\frac{1}{4}$ in. covering for tomatoes, $\frac{1}{8}$ in. for lettuce, $\frac{1}{16}$ in. for begonias) to avoid bringing light seeds to the surface again. Seed can be sown either directly from the packet, the corner of which is torn off, or better still by means of a small piece of cardboard folded down the middle. Alternatively some gardeners empty the seed into the palm of the hand and sow the seed with the fingers and thumb of the other hand. This, however, should not be adopted with very fine seed which will stick to a moist palm. Seed can also be sown in shallow drills taken out with a piece of straight cardboard, this of course only being really suitable where boxes are being used. Larger seed can be spaced out at the desired density to facilitate later handling. Always try to sow as thinly as possible, there being little virtue in thick sowing. Where compartmentised containers are used, individual sowing is desirable, but this is generally reserved for larger or pelleted seeds, the seed being merely pushed below the surface of the compost. After sowing, no matter what type of container is used, seed should be *very lightly* watered in with a *very* fine rose and covered with a sheet of glass with paper on top of this to maintain higher humidity and retain moisture. Light is unnecessary, and often undesirable, for actual germination.

GERMINATING TEMPERATURES
Ideal germinating temperatures vary according to species, but 55–60°F. will suit the majority, although some such as begonias require about 10° more. Time of germination is also extremely variable.

Seed containers should be frequently examined to see they are not dry and the glass should be turned daily to avoid droplets of moisture on the compost surface. The paper is removed *as soon as germination occurs* to avoid etiolating or drawing the little seedlings, and the glass lifted a little to allow some ventilation, until finally removed. Bright sunshine should be avoided for a few days, even if this means using a single sheet of tissue paper or other shading medium. It is interesting to note that with the now common practice

of using artificially illuminated growing rooms for commercial bedding plant production, germination is frequently
carried out in highly insulated shelved cabinets at 75° F., high
humidity being maintained with a humidifier. Germination
under these conditions can take place with many species of
bedding plants (annuals and perennials) in a few days.

PRICKING OFF
Subsequent treatment of newly germinated seedlings, no
matter how they are germinated, consists of ensuring
adequate moisture and light to induce sturdy growth until
the seedlings are large enough for pricking off into pots or
boxes, and there is much virtue in carrying this out when
the seedlings are very young to avoid checking growth by
root disturbance and crowding. (See also page 93).

The main advantage of compartmentised containers,
spaced sowing, or sowing in small peat pots, is that it avoids
pricking off checks. A stronger compost is, however, best
used to sustain the plants for the longer period, or alternatively liquid feed used timeously.

VEGETATIVE PROPAGATION
The various means of increasing plants by vegetative propagation, while tending to be confusing at first sight, follow
a constant and fairly simple pattern. Convenience and ease
of root formation play a very large part in deciding on the
best section of the plant to use, coupled of course with the
accumulated and recorded knowledge of the best propagation methods as dictated by practical experience over many
years.

Cuttings
A really sharp thin-bladed knife or a fairly new razor blade
is the first essential requisite for taking any form of cuttings.
Various sections of the plant – stems, leaves, leaf buds, or
even different sections of the leaf – may be induced to form
roots at or about the vascular system of stem or leaf. Much
can be learned about the most suitable propagation method
by investigation of the plant's growing habit, plants which
form roots near the surface of the soil being easier to pro-

pagate. A typical example is the chrysanthemum, which will be found to have a largely adventitious surface rooting system. Even the tomato, which although possessing a tap root, also forms adventitious roots at the soil surface, showing that tomatoes can in fact be readily produced from cuttings, although this is not general practice. Plants which merely form roots from the existing main tap root are more difficult to propagate.

The taking of cuttings is carried out at the appropriate time of year, this generally coinciding with a period of rapid vegetative development. The type of cutting again depends on the species involved, but generally speaking the tips of side shoots, or on occasion the terminal growth of a main branch, are selected. The selected cutting material should be representative of good balanced natural growth, neither spindly nor unduly vigorous. Soft cuttings such as those from chrysanthemums, dahlias and so on, are taken early in the year when the new season's growth has started, and these require high rooting temperatures in the order of 60–65° F.

Half-ripe cuttings. These are taken later in the year from various plants, when available, and are frequently used for pelargoniums, hydrangeas, and many other shrubs. They can be rooted at lower temperatures, possibly 50–55° F.

Ripe cuttings. Fully ripe or hard woody cuttings such as those from roses and other shrubs in the autumn, can be rooted at still lower temperatures. Modern views are, however, that higher rooting temperatures can be usefully employed for most cuttings, whether soft or fully ripe.

Cutting length depends on species, but typical cuttings are 2 to 3 in. long, with bottom leaves removed, and trimmed cleanly below a node or joint. Alternatively, as carried out in commercial practice, many cuttings can be snapped off cleanly irrespective of node position, it being claimed that this practice avoids the spread of virus or fungus diseases, sometimes introduced by knives or razor blades. At all events, every attempt should be made to avoid bruising cuttings, as this often damages the meristematic cell tissue responsible for root formation. There are, however, few definite rules about size and nature of stem cuttings, especially if there can be a happy combination of heat and high humidity to prevent wilting. Every year more is being found out about propagation, and even roses have now been found to root better from ripe stem internodal cuttings bearing 3–4 buds, with bottom heat, especially vigorous Hybrid Teas and Floribundas.

Ensuring high humidity can, of course, be achieved either by the use of a mist propagation unit or by propagating cases. Alternatively a more down to earth method is the use of polythene bags propped up with sticks over pots or boxes. Some shade is definitely necessary for the initial period, whether rooting on the open bench or in propagating cases, unless mist propagation is being practised (see page 60).

Rooting mediums vary from fine sand to equal parts of sand and peat, peat + Vermiculite, or pure peat, there being great interest now in the use of peat pellets for rooting cuttings and raising them to potting on stage without root disturbance. The cuttings are generally spaced in various containers, either boxes, seed pans, or open beds, at any convenient distance apart, generally 1 to 3 in., at a convenient depth to hold them steady, a pencil or dibble being an ideal insertion tool. There is no need to give any cuttings too much room, but at the same time they should not be needlessly crowded together.

Leaf cuttings are usually taken from Rex begonias, a large leaf being laid flat on some rooting compost after cuts have been made at various points across the leaf veins. Some gardeners lay small stones on the cuts, but this is generally unnecessary. Saintpaulia leaves are removed with the little stem or petiole attached and merely pushed into the compost up to the base of the leaf. Leaf bud cuttings are much the same, except that a section of stem bearing the small bud is left, this being one 'text book' way of propagating camellias, which of course can also be propagated from normal stem cuttings. 'Sports' from roses, chrysanthemums or other plants can also be propagated in this way. In all cases it should be noted that high humidity is still desirable, especially for leaf cuttings.

Other vegetative methods of propagation include layering, root cuttings and grafting, but these are exceptional for the average amateur gardener, except perhaps in the case of chlorophytum, where the tip of the 'flowers' are brought to the ground and pushed into the compost.

Division is also a popular method of propagation and can be carried out with many different plants which can be seen to be forming new little plants, such as *Primula obconica.* All that is required is to take the plant out of its pot, split it up into separate sections and re-pot.

Hormone rooting powder or liquid can be used with most cuttings, but always according to directions.

Greenhouse temperatures should be compatible with those of the actual rooting medium, generally in the order of 55 – 60°F. or higher, the exception being when a heated propagating case is used, as this will maintain its own temperature independent of greenhouse temperature, a practice which can be highly economical.

PRICKING OFF AND POTTING YOUNG PLANTS

Except where individual containers are used, young plants, whether raised from seed or from cuttings, should be moved on to the appropriate size of pot or box as soon as possible, and the correct time to do this will be indicated by vigorous growth of either seedlings or rooted cuttings. Where pots are to be used, which is the general practice except for the majority of bedding plants (see page 99), selecting the 'correct' size and type is not a simple matter today. The range of available pots includes clay, plastic, peat, and bituminised paper, along with soil blocks and peat pellets. Both clay and plastic pots necessitate root disturbance for the young plants when potting on or planting out, while the remainder avoid planting checks as the root ball is planted intact.

The nature of compost for pricking out or for potting will depend not only on the plant species, but also the time of year. In winter when growth is slow, and particularly for slow-growing subjects such as many rock plants or shrub seedlings, it is pointless to use more than the John Innes Seed Compost or U/C Winter Mix. Where conditions are warmer and lighter and growth, in consequence, is more vigorous, it is better to use a compost of a higher nutrient level, and the John Innes Potting Compost No. 1 or the U/C Summer Mix is ideal. Stronger composts such as the John Innes No. 2

or No. 3 are best reserved for subsequent pottings, and more especially in the height of summer for more mature plants.

Procedure for potting or pricking out involves having all material, clean or sterilised, to hand, filling boxes or containers carefully with the appropriate compost, crocking clay pots and merely putting a little roughage in the base of other types. Plastic or clay pots, after being filled to the rim, can be given a sharp bump on the bench, this usually being sufficient to firm the compost sufficiently.

The general run of bedding plants are generally put into seed trays 2 in. deep, but most other young plants are usually put into small pots of a size ranging from 2 in. for Cyclamen to $4\frac{1}{4}$ in. for tomatoes. The period of occupation in the pots, and the nature of the plant, are often the deciding factors, the object being to avoid starvation before the plants are either planted out or re-potted.

Seedlings are teased out carefully with a dibber or tally to avoid undue damage to roots or leaves, time being taken to examine the roots to see that no disease is present, and this is often indicated by a browning. The size of seedlings varies considerably, and while early pricking out is desirable, there are obvious physical limits. Some measure of selection, to grade the seedlings into size, should be practiced.

Density of seedlings in the seed box is generally 6 × 8 to give 48 per standard tray, approximate distances being indicated by going over the box area quickly with the point of a dibber, or alternatively a marker board with spaced nails can be used. A dibber is used to make the insertion hole, and the seedlings are then popped in and firmed up with the base of the dibber. When using pots or soil blocks the procedure is much the same, the exception being that with soil blocks some compost must be used to fill up the indentation. Insertion holes should always be big enough to allow entry of the seedling without undue root restriction, and depth of insertion is largely determined by common sense, it often being better to insert too deeply rather than have the seedling flopping about over the surface of the compost. Firm up and always water in after insertion, whether in boxes, pots or soil blocks. Boxes or pots should then be placed on either an open or closed bench, at a suitable temperature, generally around 60°F., and with adequate water. Many gardeners prefer to use open benches in winter when heat is important, as they claim that plants establish themselves and develop more quickly with a through current of warm air. Conversely, a closed bench is claimed to be preferable in summer to reduce watering needs.

POTTING ON AND PLANTING

The time for repotting or planting will subsequently be gauged by a combination of general vigour and root development, taking into account the appropriate time of year when planting is to be carried out, a matter which will be referred to under the respective cultural notes. Moving a plant from a smaller to a larger pot is quite a simple task and an increase in pot size of approximately 2 in. is usual, i.e. from a 3 to a 5 in. pot and so on. Pots must be clean, crocked lightly if clay, a little roughage added, and filled partly with compost, so that the plant can be removed by tapping sharply upside down from its previous pot and any crock removed, completely avoiding root ball disintegration, and then laid on top of this layer of compost with the top of the root ball $\frac{3}{4}$ in. or so below the rim of the pot. Things are a bit easier when soil blocks or peat pots are involved. In any event compost is carefully worked in around the root ball with one hand, holding the plant steady with the other. Firmness of potting depends on the type of plant and is related to general texture. Shrubby or woody species are potted firmly, soft sappy plants merely moderately. A sharp tap on the bench should finally settle the compost and plant at the right level, half an inch or so below the rim being ideal for watering purposes.

HARDENING OFF

All plants for eventual outside planting must be hardened off or acclimatised in cold frames, no matter how they are produced, and this is done by giving progressive ventilation during the day to begin with, and finally all the time during late April/May when all risk of frost is past. Strongly growing plants may be fed with a liquid fertiliser if necessary.

It is interesting to note that the use of really efficient fan ventilation can harden plants off sufficiently in the greenhouse, but this technique is only of value when everything in the greenhouse is involved, a situation common in nurseries and public parks.

LABELLING
It is good gardening practice to label boxes and pots with either a wooden, metal, or plastic label of the appropriate size.

THE USE OF ANTI-TRANSPIRANTS
The use of plastic materials for spraying on to all green material to reduce transpiration loss is a fairly new technique which is likely to become a widely accepted practice in the whole realm of propagation.

18 Raising summer bedding plants

The practice of raising young plants for summer bedding is becoming extremely popular, as although many gardeners may prefer to go along to their local nursery or garden centre and purchase what they require at remarkably reasonable prices, one has to take colour, type and quantity of plants available, and this may not always be what is required. In any case there is a real sense of achievement in raising your own plants.

TYPES OF BEDDING PLANTS
A very heterogeneous group of plants comes into the category of bedders, some perennial, some annual, some hardy, others half-hardy or tender, all of which for convenience are given the same sort of treatment, aimed at having them ready for setting out in the garden after spring displays are

Double petunias look well in window boxes, hanging baskets or other containers

'Scarlet Lustre', a grandiflora
petunia with yellow throat

PLANTS FOR SUMMER BEDDING

NAME	PROPAGATION	COLOUR	HEIGHT	DIST. APART
AGERATUM	Seeds in February/March	Blue	4–9 in.	6 in.
ALYSSUM	Seed in February/March	White, pink	4–6 in.	6 in.
ANTIRRHINUM	Seed in February/March	Various	12–18 in.	10–12 in.
ASTER	Seed in March	Various	12–18 in.	10–12 in.
BEGONIA (Fibrous rooted)	Sow seed ro take cuttings of overwintered plants in Spring	Various	9–12 in. and higher	9–12 in.
BEGONIA (Tuberous)	By division of tubers after start of growth in Spring or by seed in February/March	Various	9–12 in. or more	9–12 in.
CALCEOLARIA	By cuttings in Autumn or Spring	Red and yellow	12–15 in.	9 in.
CARNATION (Marguerite or Chabaud)	Seed by Spring. Alternatively by cuttings or by layering during previous Summer	Various	12–14 in.	12 in.
DAHLIA	Seeding in Spring for dwarf bedding types, or cuttings from overwintered tubers when growth starts. Tubers may also be planted.	Various	1-6 ft.	1–3 ft. (bedding types at 1 ft. apart)
DIANTHUS	Seed in February	Various	12–15 in.	10–12 in.
FUCHSIA	Cuttings taken in Spring	Red, pink, purple	18 in.–3 ft.	18 in.–3 ft.
GERANIUM (Zonal Pelargonum)	From cuttings taken in Spring or Autumn	Pink, white, red	9–12 in. (also trailing types)	9–12 in.
GLADIOLUS	By corms planted direct or started in heat prior to planting outside in May	Vast range of colours	1½–3 ft. or more	6–12 in.
HELIOTROPE	By cuttings taken in Spring	Blue	9 in.–3 ft.	1–3 ft.
LOBELIA	Cuttings may be taken in Spring, but usually seed is sown in February	Blue, white, pink	6–9 in.	6–9 in.
MARIGOLD (French & African)	Seed sown by February/March	Orange shades	9 in.–2½ ft.	12–15 in.

MESEMBRYAN- THEMUM	From cuttings or by seed sown in Spring	Various	Trailing	9–12 in.
MIMULUS	Seed in February/March	Yellows	12–15 in.	10–12 in.
NEMESIA	Seed in February/March	Various	9–12 in.	12 in.
NICOTIANA	Seed in February/March	Shades of white, pink etc.	12–18 in.	12 in.
PENTSTEMON	By cuttings taken in Spring or Autumn	Various	1–2 ft.	12 in.
PETUNIA	Seed in February/March	Various	12–15 in.	12 in.
PHLOX (drummondii)	Seed in Spring	Various	12–15 in.	10–12 in.
SALVIA Patens SALVIA (Scarlet)	By division cuttings in Spring Preferably by seed in February, but also by cuttings	Blue Scarlet	1½–2 ft. 1–2 ft.	10–12 in. 9 in.
TAGETES	Seed in February/March	Orange/Yellow	10–12 in.	9–12 in.
VERBENA	Cuttings in Spring or by seed in January/February	Various	Trailing	12 in.

past. Timing will therefore vary according to district, but in general mid-May is the usual time, waiting until late May in colder northern areas, or for plants which are known to be tender.

PROPAGATION METHODS

Bedding plants are raised in different ways. Some hardy and half hardy perennials are raised from cuttings taken either in the autumn around September/October before or during the lifting of plants out of their summer beds, or in the spring from plants overwintered in a frost free greenhouse (although some, such as pentstemons or marguerites, will stand frost).

Sturdy cuttings 3 to 4 in. long, preferably but not necessarily of non-flowering growth, are trimmed and placed 2 in. apart in boxes of rooting medium (sand + peat + a little clean soil). While the box can be placed in a cold frame provided either with frost protection level of heating or draped with sacks during cold weather, there is much to be said for having them in a frost free greenhouse, as winter losses can be very high during severe weather, or merely because of the excessive damp in some areas. It is neither desirable nor necessary to induce quick growth, as large plants produced too soon would merely be an embarrassment. The procedure is exactly the same with overwintered plants, but in this case the cuttings, when taken, can be encouraged to root quicker with warmth, either in boxes or on a warm propagating bench. In both instances plants must be moved when growing strongly during the early part of the year, either into good soil in a cold frame in the case of the hardier subjects such as Pentstemons, or potted individually into 4 in. pots in the case of Geraniums, using John Innes Potting Compost, U/C Summer Mix, or other suitable potting compost. They should be placed in a portion of the greenhouse where they can have plenty of light, air and space to induce strong growth.

All plants intended for outside planting are hardened off as previously described (see page 95).

DIVISION

Many plants such as centaurea or salvia can be divided in

spring after overwintering in a frost free greenhouse, and here it is merely a case of potting up the separated plants in small pots, using a good compost.

SEED
The most common way of raising bedding plants is from seed, sowing at varying times, as some species are slow in developing. A seed pan of each species generally provides a sufficient number of plants for garden use, pricking off into a variety of boxes or compartmentised containers (see page 87). Some species are bad for damping off, antirrhinums and lobelia being the chief offenders, especially where heat sterilised loam is contained in the compost and there is a subsequent release of ammonia. Soil-less media are therefore much more useful in this instance.

CUTTINGS OF TENDER PLANTS
Dahlias and begonias are typical of plants which will stand no frost at all. Cuttings are induced to grow by bedding the tubers or corms in moist peat during February and March and giving plenty of warmth, the cuttings taken being rooted normally. Overwintered Dahlia tubers and begonia corms can of course also be potted up or planted out in late April/ May when they will develop naturally.

19 Perpetual flowering carnations

For the smaller greenhouse, it is best to produce carnations on a two year basis, otherwise these plants become extremely leggy, and for that matter invariably fall prey to various diseases.

FACILITIES FOR GROWING

Good light, airy conditions are essential, with a minimum temperature of around 50° F. Plants can be grown either in 9-in. pots or in specially raised beds, 4 ft. wide, with soil raised 8 to 10 in. by slabs of concrete at the side. Drainage holes must be made in the base of the bed. The compost to use for carnations is John Innes No. 3.

CULTURAL DETAILS

Plants will generally arrive from the nursery in 3-in. pots and they should either be put into 6-in. pots with John Innes No. 3 compost or set out at 8 × 10 in. in the bed. After plants are established, remove tips to encourage side shoot development, the side shoots being stopped eventually at 5–6 in. Plants must be adequately supported either with canes if pots are being used, or if in beds with wires longitudinally secured to metal uprights and string across these. Regulars watering, even temperatures around 55–60° F., and adequate ventilation are all essential. If growing in pot move plants into 9-in. pots when they have made sufficient growth in 6–8 months.

When flower buds form, remove all but that in the centre. Feeding starts when the first flowers are cut, a well balanced fertiliser being used.

Cuttings may be taken from healthy plants for rooting in sand, so that a regular supply of new stock can be maintained.

Red Spider is the main pest (see page 156).

VARIETIES

The Sim sports are usually grown now, it being essential to obtain healthy stock at the outset.

BORDER CARNATIONS

These can also be grown in greenhouses on a short term basis by taking cuttings or layering annually and growing for one year. Use John Innes No. 2 Potting Compost and keep cool.

20 Chrysanthemums

The culture of chrysanthemums, while not necessarily restricted to greenhouses in the case of early flowering types
in most parts of Britain, cannot be divorced from the greenhouse for most mid and late-flowering types, both for cut
blooms and for propagation. For all types it is culturally
advantageous to produce new chrysanthemums from cuttings
annually, and while a frame will suffice, a greenhouse is more
accommodating.

TYPES OF CHRYSANTHEMUMS
1 Incurved – where all petals turn in to form a ball-shaped
flower.
2 Incurving – where the petals of the flowers are of looser
habit.
3 Reflexing – when petals turn outwards or droop.
4 Singles – with an eye and a single ring of petals. (Up to 5
rings for exhibition.)
5 Anemone flowering – which are single with a raised eye.
6 Large exhibition type – which have immense flowers and
are suitable for greenhouse culture only. (Can be incurved,
incurving or reflexing.)
7 Many other different types of blooms, in early, mid and
late flowering groups.

Varieties are legion and change rapidly. It is therefore
necessary to refer to a specialist chrysanthemum catalogue
or list to keep up to date. Flower Show visitation and
membership of a Chrysanthemum Society are perhaps the
best ways of keeping abreast of the newest varieties and cultural techniques.

It is important to start off with good reliable stock, and
thereafter maintain strict supervision to avoid stock deterioration due to the spread of disease by various means.
The best time to select propagation stock is when the plants
are in full flower, rejecting any plants which show signs of
weak growth, mottled leaves, or flower distortion.

SOME BASIC FACTS ABOUT THE CHRYSANTHEMUM

Chrysanthemums generally (other than some early varieties) are photoperiodic plants and will only initiate their flower buds when the day length is less than $14\frac{1}{2}$ hours (see also page 108). They are perennial in nature and the modern varieties have a remarkably hardy root stock (the part below ground). The flowers and foliage can stand fairly low temperatures, much depending on type and variety. Chrysanthemums will grow between spring and autumn (from May until September) out of doors, and with modern lighting and shading techniques can be induced to grow and flower under glass at any time of the year.

FACILITIES FOR GROWING

These centre around a well designed light admitting greenhouse with a heating system capable of maintaining a temperature of at least 45–50°F. for autumn and winter flowering and for propagation. A frame is desirable for hardening off, as is a slatted or capillary bench for pot grown types. There are now three main modes of greenhouse culture (excluding year-round or 'spot' culture, where lighting and shading is employed). These are:
1 Growing continually in pots,
2 Growing in borders out of doors for lifting into the greenhouse,
3 Direct planting in greenhouse borders.

There is of course also outside culture of chrysanthemums, when the plants, although they may be greenhouse raised, will flower out of doors.

PROPAGATION FOR POT GROWING OR 'LIFTERS'

Times of propagation are as follows:
1 Large exhibition greenhouse varieties in December and January.
2 Late flowering and mid-season varieties in February and March.
3 Early flowering types in March and April.

Propagation material should be selected from stools overwintered in protected frames or frost free greenhouses. Short growths are selected which are $\frac{1}{8}$ in. in diameter and 2–3 in.

long. The cuttings should preferably be taken below a joint, but this is not essential, and the lower leaves are always removed. After dipping the cuttings in hormone powder, insert them $\frac{1}{2}$ to $\frac{3}{4}$ in. deep in seed trays at a distance of $1-1\frac{1}{2}$ in. apart, using a rooting medium of equal parts finely riddled peat and sand, or, for later propagation, John Innes Seed Compost. The cuttings should be well watered in and given a temperature of 55–60° F. Rooting generally takes place in 14 to 30 days, according to variety, with an average of 21 days, although on mist propagation benches rooting can be achieved very much quicker. Polythene bags placed over the top of the boxes will create humidity and hasten rooting. Cuttings may wilt for the first few days, but shading with newspaper will help to prevent this. An alternative to box rooting is rooting directly into peat pellets, the cuttings being inserted individually, and there is much virtue in this method.

POTTING
Cuttings, when rooted, as can be seen by freshening tip growth, can either be potted into 3 in. pots of clay, plastic or peat, filled with a good potting compost, generally John Innes Potting No. 1, or alternatively later taken cuttings can be planted out 5 × 5 in. apart in good rich soil in a cold frame. Pot firmly and carefully, giving the plants plenty of light and keep them merely moist to induce hard growth.

STOPPING OR PINCHING
The practice of stopping or pinching is carried out with all but the Spray types. This is done by removing the top of the single stems completely, avoiding bruising of tissue, and is carried out when 6 to 9 in. of growth has developed and buds are seen to be breaking. It results in the formation of side shoots. It is important *not* to stop a plant simultaneously with potting or planting out, and with pot grown types it is generally carried out after either the second potting according to growth rate, while with outside planted types, it takes place after they have recovered from the shock of planting, generally around the first week of June. The number of stems allowed to remain often depends on purpose.

OUTDOOR PLANTING
Plants intended for outdoor culture, or 'lifters', should be placed in a cold frame and hardened off ready for planting outside in early or mid-May. Planting distances for cut flower production are 12 × 14 in. apart in a 3 to 4 ft. wide bed. Earlies for dwarf bedding culture can be planted a little closer, around 12 × 12 in. For 'lifters' a little more space may be given, up to 18 in. apart. Support must be given, either with individual canes or netting strained to posts. Early dwarf types require no support.

GROWING IN POTS
Plants in 3-in. pots are moved on to 5-in. pots, checking that the roots are well through the ball by careful inspection. This is done by holding the pot upside down and allowing the root ball to drop into the hand. Use John Innes No. 2 compost and crock clay pots, putting plenty of roughage in the bottom of the pot. Pot all plants firmly.

FINAL POTTING
The final potting is into 8- or 9-in. pots, using plenty of roughage and John Innes No. 3 compost. Plants *must* be potted very firmly, using, if necessary, a potting stick. Three strong 4 to 5 ft. canes are then inserted around the edge of the pot and the plants are supported by strong twine around the canes, later of course tying the number of stems allowed to form individually to each cane. Place pots in a square for a few days to give natural protection and then put them in a line, keeping the pots 6 in. apart, or on outside beds or gravel paths *not* recently treated with weedkiller. Keep them entirely level and tie at least one cane in each pot to a strong fence erected with posts and wires. Plants should be fed and watered regularly, and pots given a twist occasionally to prevent rooting into base.

DISBUDDING
Disbudding should be carried out regularly (except for Spray varieties) leaving the centre or terminal bud in each case, unless specific recommendations are given to the contrary with any variety.

LIFTING IN

Plants are generally lifted into the greenhouse in September or early October before any heavy frosts occur. The greenhouse is kept fully ventilated for a few weeks, no heat being necessary at this stage, and thereafter heat is given at the 45–50° F. level. Watering and feeding is continued, particular attention also being paid to pest and disease control, especially mildew, which can be largely prevented by adequate ventilation.

LIFTED PLANTS ('LIFTERS')

Before lifting plants in, greenhouse borders are forked over, but do not generally require much more attention, especially if a crop of tomatoes has been grown. Generally, however, 4 to 6 oz. per sq. yd. of a good general fertiliser should be applied. The pH of the soil should also be adjusted to 6.5. Plants are lifted with a sharp spade, it sometimes being advisable to cut around the roots a fortnight or a week before. They are lifted with as large a root ball as possible, placed in the greenhouse border fairly tightly, and thoroughly watered in. Some wilting may occur, but if the greenhouse is kept cool the plants quickly recover. Some varieties will, of course, lift better than others. Heat is given after a couple of weeks at the 45–50° F. level.

DIRECT PLANTING

Widely practiced by commercial growers, this system avoids a great deal of the summer attention required out of doors. Nevertheless, it also restricts the use of greenhouse borders for tomatoes (other than for a very early crop) and other crops. Under greenhouse conditions chrysanthemums usually grow much more quickly than they do out of doors, and the growing season can therefore be considerably shortened. Planting may take place from June to mid-August with natural illumination. The problem, however, is that while it is simple for the commercial grower to obtain rooted cuttings in quantity for direct planting from specialist raisers, it is difficult for the amateur to obtain merely a few plants. It may of course be possible to get a few cuttings from a commercial grower if these are ordered early enough. Alternatively cuttings are taken early in the year, when available, and planted in the greenhouse border at a distance of 9 × 9 in. apart. These are then stopped when they are growing vigorously by pinching out the tops, and in due course cuttings are taken again and rooted. These provide the young plants for setting out in a well-prepared greenhouse border which has been dressed with lime to give a pH of 6.5, and a compound fertiliser at 6 to 8 oz. per sq. yd.

PLANTING
If planting between June and early July from self-raised or bought plants, allow 10 × 10 in. or 9 × 9 in., if mid to late July allow 7 × 8 in., and for planting up to around the third week of August, allow 5 × 5 in. and take only *one* stem (without stopping). It helps to give even growth if plants are 'graded' into sizes when planting. Beds should be approximately 4 ft. 6 in. to 5 ft. wide.

STOPPING
Plants generally make rapid growth under warm greenhouse conditions, and stopping is carried out a week or so after planting for all but the single stem crop. Regular watering is essential, as also is liquid feeding, the emphasis being on potash or nitrogen, according to whether growth is soft or hard respectively. Support is best achieved by means of 6 in. mesh netting of either hessian or plastic strained on supports, and this is gradually raised as the plants grow. Stringent pest and disease control is essential, and adequate ventilation should be given constantly, maintaining temperatures in the 55–60°F. region, especially during bud formation time around September and October.

Flowering period will extend from October until Xmas, or later according to variety, this depending on what is called the response group. This is a technique invaluable for the cut flower enthusiast, but it will be found that a little practical experience is worth a great deal. Both standard and spray varieties can of course be grown. Apart from cut flowers, pots of dwarf spray chrysanths can be grown on the same principle, 3 to 5 plants per 6-in. plastic half-pot, following much the same timing.

ALL YEAR ROUND CHRYSANTHEMUMS

Based on the principle that certain chrysanths only form their flower buds when the daylight is less than 14½ hours, this is also a technique which is widely practised commercially. Both bed and pot culture can be practised, in the first case in 5 ft. wide beds, in the same manner as described for direct planting, and for pot culture on either open or capillary type benches, usually 5 young plants being planted per 6–9 in. 'half-pot' or seed pan. The border soil must be of good quality and regularly changed or steam sterilised, not only to avoid disease but to reduce build-up of chemicals or plant toxins. This can in fact create cultural difficulties for the amateur, as chemical sterilisation is not often feasible for a number of reasons. With pots John Innes No. 2 or U/C Summer Mix should always be used. Temperature must be accurately controlled in the region of 55–60° F. if growth is to be maintained. Facilities must also be available for a line of 60 watt tungsten filament lights centrally situated over the beds at a height of 5 ft., (4 ft. apart) and also a framework of wires for supporting black polythene shading, so that by either lighting or shading the plants the photoperiodic impulse can be adjusted according to the time of year to either induce the plant to develop vegetatively (by simulating a day length of more than 14½ hours) and initiating flower buds by bringing it below 14½ hours by shading.

Important note: It is emphasised that all-the-year-round culture of chrysanthemums including 'spot' cropping, is a highly specialised technique well outwith the scope of this book, and gardeners deeply interested are urged to consult a specialist work on the subject. (See also Chapter 10).

21 Bulb forcing

21 Bulb forcing

The forcing of bulbs, while not exclusively a greenhouse task, is a sphere of culture which offers very wide scope. For the earliest flowers, specially prepared bulbs are obtained and planted tightly in bowls with bulb fibre with the nose of the bulb showing, or in pots or boxes with fresh soil (which has not previously grown bulbs), planting hyacinths in September and tulips or daffodils in October. Rooting occurs best under low temperatures and this can be readily achieved under a thick insulating layer of moist peat in a sheltered corner of the garden or a vacant cold frame. Further watering is seldom required unless the weather is exceptionally dry, when the peat should be thoroughly hosed.

Bulbs are lifted into a warm greenhouse at a temperature of 55–60°F. when growing shoots are well extended, i.e. 1½–2 in., or, in the case of daffodils, when the flower bud can be felt clear of the neck of the bulb. Keep tulips and hyacinths dark at first, daffodils light, and eventually after 7–10 days when flowers stems are well extended, give more heat and full light. This can be discontinued for later flowering, the bulbs being brought straight into light. Always ensure that the bulbs do not dry out.

Bowls of bulbs can of course be treated in the dwelling house in exactly the same way, or alternatively they can be given the necessary dark treatment in the greenhouse before lifting into the dwelling house for actual flowering.

FLOWERING IN ARTIFICIAL LIGHT
Bulbs, tulips, hyacinths and daffodils, can be flowered after the same treatment in warm cellars or cupboards at 65–70°F., with artificial lighting, a 100 watt bulb being used for every sq. yd., and operated 12 hours in each 24, the tulips and hyacinths having been given a period of darkness prior to forcing. Daffodils may tend to produce excess foliage under low intensity artificial lighting, especially if temperatures are too high. As has been stated previously, much more interest is now being shown in the whole realm of growing under artificial light (see Chapter 10).

BORDER GROWING
In addition, of course, bulbs, especially tulips and daffodils, can be planted up closely in greenhouse borders to provide early cut flowers at appropriate times of the year.

Crocus is also a useful flower for greenhouse culture, being planted in pots in October.

GLADIOLI

These beautiful corms can be induced to flower very much earlier than they would out of doors by planting in well prepared borders 3 in. deep at a distance apart of 6 × 6 in. in February or March. The primulinus type is much more popular for this purpose and Allard Pierson is also an excellent early flowering type.

IRIS

Iris also, especially the varieties 'Wedgewood' and 'Imperator', can be grown in much the same way as gladioli for early bloom, and can also be planted in the autumn for spring flowering, preferably in greenhouse borders 3 in. deep and 3–4 in. apart.

FREESIAS

These are most attractive cut flowers for home decoration and, because of modern breeding, they are now available in a wonderful range of colours. They can be grown either from seed or from corms, the seed being sown in April and the corms planted in September.

There are three main ways of growing from seed. The first method is to sow the seed in boxes of moist peat, covered with a sheet of glass and paper, maintaining a temperature of 55–60°F, and pricking off the little seedlings 2 in. apart into 9 in. pots of clay or bituminised paper filled with John Innes No. 2 or U/C Summer Mix compost. Alternatively the seed can be sown direct in the containers, although germination tends to be erratic. Another method is to sow the seed individually into peat blocks, for planting either into pots or greenhouse borders, although this is likely to be less attractive to the amateur as it takes up great greenhouse space and the plants also tend to make a lot of foliage at the expense of flowers. The young plants in boxes or pots are taken outside to stand in a vacant cold frame during the summer, where, if fed and watered regularly, they will make good growth. Plants are lifted into the greenhouse in September when, if given water and moderate warmth, they will soon flower, and continue to produce blooms over a long period. Support with twigs or nets will be necessary to avoid the plants flopping hopelessly.

22 Pot plant cultivation

Britain, unfortunately, still lags behind many Continental countries as far as indoor decor with pot plants is concerned. Many of the homes in Holland, for example, have large picture windows full of the most magnificent galaxy of plants one can imagine. Inherent appreciation over generations for all things which grow has, I feel, for a large proportion of the population, much to do with this philosophy. Nevertheless, it merely needs a start with pot plants, when, with a little experience, I feel sure that many gardeners could emulate our Continental neighbours.

Much of the success in pot plant culture lies in a happy blend of patience and common sense. The greenhouse should be considered both as the production unit to provide a range of pot plants over the year for the home, and as an absorbing and attractive feature on its own.

WHAT DOES ONE NEED TO GROW POT PLANTS?
A well-situated, adequately ventilated, drip-free greenhouse, with a good clean water supply and a heating system capable of maintaining a temperature of around 50–55°F. is the first essential. There must also be a good system of benching, either on one level or tiered, not only to make more use of space, but to present a more attractive appearance. A convenient corner of a bench, either in the greenhouse or in a nearby shed, should be available for potting activities, and there must also be a storage area for the ingredients necessary for growing mediums, although these days, with easily

bought, reliably formulated mixtures, this is not now so essential. There should also be suitable storage space for pots and seed boxes. It is also necessary to think of propagation facilities in the form of either a propagating case or a temporary or 'permanent' rooting bench.

PLANT RAISING
Methods of propagation will depend upon what is considered to be the most effective technique. Where vegetative methods are used, it will be necessary to obtain stock plants or beg a cutting or two, while for seed sowing it is simply a question of deciding what to start with and making the necessary purchases. Some plan of action will, however, be necessary, preferably starting off at the appropriate time of year in the prescribed manner (see Chapter 17). The methods of seed sowing, cutting selection and rooting, leaf propagation, etc., are matters which were referred to earlier, as also were the appropriate composts for satisfactory growth.

SOME GENERAL RULES IN PLANT TREATMENT
Plants vary greatly in their growing habits, growing vegetatively and flowering at different times of the year. Success lies in sustaining healthy growth by choosing the correct size of pot, so that plants are neither over nor under potted, selecting the correct compost for each stage, and, perhaps most important of all, providing the necessary water and nutrients in a well controlled environment, liquid feeding being considered necessary every 10–14 days with most actively growing pot plants, except cacti and slow growing plants such as ferns. It would be foolish to pretend that one can start with pot plant culture and achieve 100% success with no set-backs. It would also be equally misleading to assume that there is any substitute for practical experience over a period. Nevertheless, if there is a common sense approach from the start, then I feel sure that success will far outweight failure.

THE RANGE OF PLANTS TO BE GROWN
The number of different types of pot plants which can be grown in a frost free greenhouse is legion, but I would suggest that in the beginning at any rate, the more simple types are

Zinnias, so useful for cutting or
bedding, have a wide colour range

The popular *Philodendron cordatum*
is naturally a trailing vine

selected. Plants such as primulas, pelargoniums, coleus, fuchsia, and many annuals, make excellent pot plants and are relatively simple to grow, while others such as tuberous begonias, cinerarias, or streptocarpus can be a little more difficult. Many cacti are the essence of simplicity.

Annuals in pots
In addition to the flowering plants dealt with, a great many annuals can be grown in the greenhouse as pot plants, or in borders, to give a bright show of colour and provide cut flowers. Some of the best for these purposes are:

Acrolinum,	Larkspur,
Antirrhinum (actually a perennial)	Nasturtium,
Arctotis,	Nemesia,
Calendula,	Petunia,
Felicia,	Ursinia,
Godetia,	Zinnia.

Sow seed in March/April and pot into 3 in. pots. All merely require moderate heat.

Orchids
There is great interest today in the cultivation of Orchids, many of which require merely a frost free greenhouse, as distinct from those which need almost stove conditions. Humidity and shade during the summer are essential for all types. The basic compost for Orchids is equal parts of sphagnum moss and osmunda fibre with a little bit of broken crock worked through to give good drainage. I would suggest that any gardener contemplating the culture of Orchids would do well to consult a specialist book on the subject, or become a member of one of the Orchid Societies.

Alpines
As diverse a range of alpine plants as one could imagine will grow excellently in the cool greenhouse. This again tends to be a more specialised sphere and information on the culture of alpines in cool greenhouses is readily obtainable through membership of Alpine Societies or Rock Garden Clubs.

FERNS
A wide range of Ferns can be grown in a greenhouse, preferably cool, shady and moist, a north facing greenhouse being ideal. These can be propagated in a variety of ways from runners to seeds. The following is a list of some suitable varieties:

Adiantum cuneatum	*Pteris cretica major*
Adiantum decorum	*Pteris wimsettii*
Adiantum elegans	*Pteris cretica albolineata*
Cyrtomium falcatum (Holly fern)	*Pteris tremula*

Ferns from bulbils (similar to small bulbs).
The only species grown as a pot plant is Asplenium bulbiferum.

Ferns from runners
The best type for this treatment is the Nephrolepis varieties, where the little plants are attached to a parent plant and are merely pegged down and allowed to root.

OTHER POT PLANTS
In addition to the plants so far mentioned, a vast range of shrub and herbaceous plants can be potted and induced to flower much earlier than they would out of doors. The list of these is endless and includes virtually every shrub and plant of reasonable size.

Wall plants and shrubs
Many tender wall plants and shrubs are ideal for a conservatory or lean-to greenhouse, the best of which are as follows:

Cobaea scandens	*Jasminum*
Ipomea rubro-caerulea	*Plumbago capensis*
Bougainvillea	

HANGING BASKETS
While hanging baskets are frequently used for outside work, the plants to fill them are invariably produced in a greenhouse. In addition, hanging baskets strategically placed in the

larger greenhouse or conservatory can give a wonderful effect. Baskets can be of wire or plastic and of various sizes, generally 12 to 14 in. in diameter. The older way of filling baskets was first of all to line them with moss, then fill with good compost, pushing the odd small plant, such as trailing Lobelia through the wire at the side, and finally setting a selection of plants in the basket, taller types in the centre, trailing types around the edges. Nowadays it is usual to line the basket with green polythene, which can be bought of the correct shape and size specifically for this purpose. The selection of plants which can be grown is legion, the following being the most *popular*:

Achimenes
Ageratum
Alyssum
Aubrieta
Begonias – tuberous and fibrous
Campanula isophylla
Fuchsia
Gazania splendens
Hoya bella
The Ivies

Lachenalia bulbifera
Marguerite
Pelargoniums
Phlox drummondi
Trailing geraniums
Trailing lobelia
Verbena
Zygocactus truncatus
and many others.

FLOWERING PLANTS

SPECIES	VARIETY	EASE OF CULTURE	PROPAGATION	FLOWERING TIME	AVER. HEIGHT	TEMP. REQ.	NOTES
ACHIMENES	various colours	T	Rhizomes (tubers) March/April	May–Sept.	6–9 in.	I	Dry out rhizomes over winter
APHELANDRA	squarrosa louisae	T	Cuttings, various times. Use propagation case	Various	12–16 in.	H	Can be difficult to grow and dislike damp or draughts
AZALEA	indica	D	Cuttings in Spring in propagating case	Xmas on	12–16 in.	C/I	Grafted plants can be retained for years if plunged in outside soil during Summer and repotted in lime-free soil in Autumn
BELOPERONE	Guttata (Shrimp Plant)	D	Cuttings in April in propagating case	Summer	12–16 in.	I	Likes a little shade in summer. Give plenty of water
BEGONIA	Semperflorens	T	Seed Feb./onwards	June–Sept.	6–12 in.	I	Tubers rest in winter
	Tuberous (double)	E	Start tubers February	June–Sept.	12–15 in.	I	
	Gloire de Lorraine	E	Cuttings mid-August Cuttings Feb./onwards	November–February	9–12 in.	I	
CACTI	various types	E/T	Various methods. Sections of stems etc., also seed	Various	Various	C/I	Dozens of different types. Most can be grown in frost-free green house in J.I. + grit. Give plenty of sun
CALCEOLARIA	herbeohybrida (hybrida multiflora) multiflora nana	T T	Seed in July/August	March–May	12–16 in.	C	Cool steady growth. Put in 5–6 in. pots for flowering
CAMELLIA	japonica	D	Leaf bud cuttings March. Pot in 6 in. pots	Winter/Early Spring	18–24 in. (as p. p.)	C	Lime-free compost essential. Stand in cold frame in summer
CAMPANULA	isophylla alba	E	Cuttings in March	Summer	Pendulous	C	Ideal for hanging baskets or edge of staging
CAPSICUM (grown for decorative fruit)	annuum	T	Seed in February	Autumn on	10–12 in.	C	Keep cool. Shade if necessary. Spray frequently when flowering to assist fruit formation
CELOSIA	argentea cristata pyramidalis	E	Seed in February	May–Sept.	15 in.	C	A reasonably simple plant to grow. Gives good colour and lots of interest

CHRYSANTHEMUMS (in pots)		See Chapter 20					
CINERARIA	grandiflora, multiflora, multiflora nana	T	Seed May–June	Spring on	12–15 in.	C	Place outside in summer in shaded position. Keep cool in greenhouse not above 55°F. Best on slatted open bench
CRASSULA	Rochea coccinea	E	Cuttings in Spring	June on	9–10 in.	C	Add lime to compost. Cold frames in Summer
CYCLAMEN	persicum	D	Seed space sown (120 seeds per tray) September–January. Pot early and keep corm above soil level. Corms can be potted in August	August on	9–10 in.	C	Flowers in 5–6 in. pot. Cold frame or cool greenhouse in Summer. Regular feeding essential
ECHEVARIA	retusa	E	Sections of stem with rosette of leaves after flowering	Winter	9–10 in.	C/I	A relatively easy plant to grow, but dislikes overwatering
ERICA (Heath)	gracilis, gracilis alba, nivalis, hyemalis, willmorei	T	Tip of stem cuttings, $\frac{3}{4}$ in. long. in November–January. Root in 3 parts peat, 1 part sand in propagating case	Throughout Winter	12–18 in.	C	Lime-free compost (J.I. + flowers of sulphur, without lime). Stop frequently to encourage bushy growth. Takes 2 years to develop. Plant outside during second season
FUCHSIA	fulgens (many different varieties)	E	Internodal cuttings January/February in individual containers. Root in propagating case	Summer/ Autumn	Various	C	Frequent feeding essential. Give plenty of air and water in later stages of growth. Stake Bad for fly
GENISTA	(cytisus canariensis)	E	Cuttings January/April. Takes 2 years to produce good plant	Spring	12–24 in.	C	Really a shrub. Merely requires cool growing and regular trimming to keep bushy. Stand outside and keep shaded during second season. Lift in for Winter

		E		Long flowering period	Various	C	
GERANIUM	(Zonal Pelargonium) (Regal Pelargonium) Many lovely varieties, the newer Irene strain being especially floriferous. Ivy-leaved, especially for hanging baskets. Scented – variegated	E	Cuttings at various times of year. Autumn or Spring. Individual containers or open propagating bench		Various	C	One of the easiest plants to grow. Do not overwater and keep feeding
GLOXINIA	(amaryllis)	T	Seed in January–February. Tubers, leaf cuttings Mid-April in propagating case	August/September	9–12 in.	I	Requires constant watering and feeding
HIPPEASTRUM	(amaryllis)	T	Pot bulb in 5–6 in. pot for starting in Spring. December or earlier	Xmas/Spring	18–20 in	I	
HYDRANGEA	macrophylla (Many excellent varieties)	D	Internodal stem cuttings February/May (non-flowering shoots only). Trim leaves to reduce transpiration loss	Spring	16–20 in. or taller	C/I	Stand outside in Summer, or in cold frame. Pinch plant to encourage leaf growth. Keep Nitrogen and Phosphate levels low during feeding. Use Iron Sequestrine if foliage turns white. Apply blueing compound to intensify blue colour
IMPATIENS	sultanii (Busy Lizzie)	E	Seed February/March or cuttings at various times	Summer	10–15 in.	C/I	A very simple plant to grow. Must have plenty of light
MARGUERITE	(Crysanthemum frutescens) (white) (C. coronarium (yellow))	E	Cuttings August/January. Seed February	Summer	12–16 in.	C	Keep cool. Stop frequently to induce bushy plant
POINSETTIA	euphorbia pulcherima	D	Stem cuttings in May	Autumn/Winter	2–4 ft.	C/I	Stand in frame August/September and avoid dryness. Grown for coloured bracts

Name	Type	Sowing/Propagation	Flowering	Height	Temp.	Notes
POLYANTHUS	E	Seed in May. Pot into 3½ in. pots	Early Spring on	9–12 in.	C	Stand in frame during Summer. Keep cool and well watered. Lift into greenhouse December onwards
PRIMULA	E	Seed sown thickly May–June. Pot into 5 in. pot	Spring/Summer	9–12 in.	C	Keep dry in winter till flowering starts. Apply iron sequestrine if yellowing of foliage occurs. Note: Many people are allergic to Primulas, (causes a rash)
obconica malacoides kewensii sineusis						
ROSES	T	Buy in and pot in 5 in. pots December/January and cut hard back	Summer	16–18 in.	C/I	The object is merely to advance flowering. Use any good compost and keep feeding
Dwarf types						
SAINTPAULIA	T	Seed in Spring (do not come true from seed). Leaf stalk cuttings. Shade from direct light	Flower over a long period	6–9 in.	I/H	Feed regularly with high potash feed. Keep well watered and warm. Avoid draughts
ionantha						
SALPIGLOSSIS	T	Seed in September	May	2–3 ft.	C	Grow cool
SALVIA	E	Seed in January/February. Flowers in 5 in. pot	Summer	9–12 in.	C	Really a bedding plant, but excellent in pots. Keep cool in Summer
Blaze of Fire, Harbinger						
SCHIZANTHUS	T	Seed August	April/May	12–24 in.	C	Grow cool. Give plenty of light and adequate support. Pinch out to ensure bushy growth
(Poor Man's Orchid)						
SOLANIUM	D	Seed in February. Sow 150 per tray. Cuttings in February in propagating case	Winter especially Xmas	12–16 in.	I	Stand in shady frames in summer, lifting out during September. Always add Epsom Salts, ¾ oz. per bushel. Stop plant height to induce bushy growth. Syringe frequently during flowering to induce setting. Save seed of good forms
capsicastrum, pseudocapsicum (attractive berries)						

STOCKS	Beauty of Nice	E	Seed July/August	Spring		C	Keep cool and airy
STREPTOCARPUS		T	Seed January/March. Leaf cuttings in August	August/October		C	Feed and water regularly
ZANTEDESCHIA	aethiopica Arum (Easter Lily)	T	Division in July/August	Easter on	2–3 ft.	C/I	Rest outdoors in Summer before repotting
ZYGOCACTUS	truncatus (Xmas Cactus) syn-epiphyllum	E	Sections of stem segments in Spring	Xmas on	pendulous	C	Keep cool in summer. Give plenty of water. Repot occasionally

SPECIES	VARIETY	PROPAGATION	HEIGHT	TEMP	NOTES
ARALIA (Fatsia)	fastsia japonica	Root cuttings in March	2–3 ft.	C	Green healthy fig-like leaves
BEGONIA	Rex (Many other types)	Leaf or stem cuttings anytime in propagating case	12–24 in. and taller	I	Water sparingly in Winter
CHLOROPHYTUM	comosum variegatum (Spider Plant)	Layer small plantlets to ground	12–18 in.	C	Easy plant to grow
CISSUS (Kangaroo Vine)	antartica, striata	Leaf bud or terminal cuttings	12–18 in.	I	An excellent foliage plant. Keep well supported
COLEUS	blumei (Many varieties and colour forms)	Seed – Variable colours. Cuttings rooted in propagating case in Spring	1–2 ft.	I	Must have plenty of light. Keep well watered
CROTON	Codiaeum variegatum	Cuttings with at least 6–7 leaves. Also leaf bud cuttings. Both in propagating case	1–2 ft.	I	Give full light and keep cool. Shade only in full sun.
DIEFFENBACHIA	picta (Dumb Cane)	Terminal and stem cuttings, the latter with 2 buds horizontally. Both in propagating case	1–2 ft.	I	A fairly easy plant to grow
DRACAENA	(inc. Cordyline)	Steam and leaf bud cuttings, also toes (underground stems) in propagating case for Mahmoud Bey and W. H. Taylor. Cordyline australis and C. terminalis from seed February/March	18 in.	I	Shade and high humidity necessary
FATSHEDERA	(a cross between Fatsia japonica and Hedera helex)	Terminal and leaf bud cuttings in propagating case	18–24 in.	I	Must be well supported
FICUS	elastica decora, lyrata (Fiddle-leaf fig) pumila	Leaf bud and terminal cuttings in propagating case	1–2 ft.	I/H	Not the easiest plant to grow
GREVILLEA	robusta (Silk Oak)	Seed November/March	2 ft.	I	Cool and shade required
HEDERA	(The Ivies)	Tips or leaf cuttings anytime	Trailing	I	Easy to grow. Ideal for edge of staging

Genus	Species / variety	Propagation	Size	C/I	Notes
MARANTA	leuconeura kerchoviana	Division of roots in Spring	1–2 ft.	I	An easily grown plant
PEPEROMIA	argyreia (sandersii) hederifolia	Leaf bud cuttings or leaf blade sections	9–12 in.	I	An easy plant to cultivate
	tithymaloides 'variegata'	Leaf bud or terminal stem cuttings. All in propagating case			
PHILODENDRON	(Various species which include a number of related plants such as Scindapsus aureus and Montstera deliciosa)	Leaf bud cuttings in propagating case	12–16 in.	I	Require support. Shade from sun
PILEA	cadeiri	Nodal or terminal cuttings in propagating case	9–12 in.	I	An easy plant to grow
RHOICISSUS	rhomboidea (Grape Ivy)	Leaf bud or heeled cuttings in propagating case	12–24 in.	I	Requires support
RICINUS	communis (Castor Oil Plant), (red) gibsonii, (red) sanguinea, (green) zanzibarensis	Seed in February/March	2–3 ft.	I	Give plenty of light
SANSEVIERIA	trifasciata (Mother-in-Law's Tongue or Bowstring Hemp)	Cuttings from leaf tip or suckers (variegated types)	16–18 in.	I	An indestructible plant. Easy to grow
SAXIFRAGA	stolonifera (Mother-of-Thousands)	Runners, root separating, or from seed		C	One of the easiest plants to grow
SELAGINELLA	(Many different types)	Cuttings	4–6 in.	I	A useful plant for greenhouse staging
TRADESCANTIA	(Various varieties including Zebrina – Wandering Sailor)	Cuttings	Trailing	I	Easily grown plant with variegated leaves. Ideal for edge greenhouse staging

23 Tomatoes

The growing of tomatoes in a greenhouse is both interesting and rewarding. Any reasonably well designed greenhouse will grow tomatoes, the best results being obtained where light conditions and environmental control are optimal. Obviously, therefore, better yields can be expected in a greenhouse (and a district) where light intensity is high, but perfectly acceptable crops can be produced in most parts of Britain. Unfortunately cultural techniques in recent years have tended to diversify to such an extent that many gardeners have become confused.

SYSTEMS OF CULTURE
1 **Border culture**, where the plants are grown in the actual border soil of the greenhouse.

Advantages: Less general attention is required, with reduced watering and feeding needs.

Disadvantages: Successive crops in the same soil deteriorate due to 'soil sickness' which is caused by a manifestation of fungal and virus diseases, along with a change in bacterial activity. Coupled with this, a build-up of fertiliser residues and plant toxins can occur. This necessitates either soil sterilisation or soil renewal, the former now being effectively achieved chemically with metham sodium (see Chapter 14). The control of excess vigour can also be difficult when plants are border grown. Another disadvantage is that soil in borders can be very slow to warm up in the spring, frequently resulting in checks to roots at planting time.

2 **Grafted plants in borders.** Here normal varieties are grafted on to root stocks presently possessing various resistances to fungal diseases and root knot eelworm (NOT potato root eelworm). The process of grafting is simply achieved by a splice graft and Scotch tape, performed when both plants are removed from their pots when 6 to 8 in. tall, the top portion of the root stock being removed when the plants are being repotted. They are eventually planted out, with or without both roots (preferably with both roots to

avoid checks). While the same general disadvantages of border culture apply, continued vigour of plants on grafts right to the end of the season is excellent, and it would appear that the various problems associated with monoculture can be very effectively overcome. Grafted plants can be bought from nurserymen at approximately twice the price of conventional plants.

3 Ring culture. This system of culture involves the growing of plants in containers, generally 9 in. bituminised pots or rings, on top of a 4–6 in. layer of weathered ashes, gravel, or other inert material.

Advantages: Only limited quantities of fresh or sterilised soil are required annually to ensure a clean start. Control of growth can be readily achieved, especially early in the season, due to limited area of root development; the limited quantity of growing medium is naturally fully exposed to sun and warmth from heating systems, and can be quickly raised to the desired planting temperature (56–57°F.), thus avoiding checks to growth. (Note that it cools more quickly too.)

Disadvantages: As border soil is partly removed or covered, this is not then available for other crops, although chrysanthemums can be grown on ring culture. Watering and feeding require constant attention, especially early in the year before roots gain access to the aggregate. It is also a simple matter to upset the nutritional balance of the small quantity of soil.

4 Growing in limited quantities of growing medium. A variety of methods are involved here, ranging from boxes of soil to polythene buckets containing peat and vermiculite, the spreading of layers of soil or peat/sand on top of polythene, or the use of bituminised paper rings on top of polythene and surrounding the rings with a 2–3 in. layer of peat or growing medium.

Advantages and disadvantages are in much the same categories as for ring culture, with the exception that constant attention to watering will be required for the full season, whereas in ring culture watering is seldom such a problem once the root system develops freely into the aggregate.

5 Straw bale culture. Full, half or even quarter bales of straw laid on polythene to act as a pest and disease barrier, and fermented with chemicals, forms the basis for this method, the plants being set out on a layer of growing medium placed along the top of the bales.

Advantages: A clean start annually; no planting checks due to the great amount of warmth generated by the fermenting straw; extra CO_2 given off by decaying straw assists growth of plants.

Disadvantages: Bales are bulky and take up a lot of space in a small greenhouse, although the use of sections of bales helps here; Vigour control can be difficult, as roots develop freely; Constant watering is necessary, both initially to thoroughly soak the bales during fermentation, and during the growing season.

6 Single or double truss cropping: Still in its infancy, this system usually involves the growing of closely set plants to one or two trusses only in tiered troughs which are automatically fed and watered. A compromise is to give plants a spacing of 9 × 9 in. apart in borders and take them to one or two trusses only. It is doubtful whether this system will, as yet, hold much interest for the amateur gardener, and indeed it has still to be proved viable in commercial circles.

TOMATO GROWING TIME TABLE
It is, I feel, important to realise that type of greenhouse, efficiency of heating system, and of course locality, will all have a large part to play in deciding when to start with a crop of tomatoes. Only the really specialist gardener with a very well equipped greenhouse in a good light area should attempt the earliest crop. The majority of gardeners will find that mid-March – mid/late April planting will perhaps not only meet their purposes, but also their pocket in respect of heating costs.

PROGRAMME FOR TOMATO GROWING

Sowing Date	Planting Date	First Fruits Ripe
Late November	Mid February	Mid/End April (really early crops should only be

attempted in a good light
area with first class facilities).

Early December	Late February	April–May
Late Dec/Early January	Mid Mar/Early April	Early/Mid May
Mid/late February	Late April	June/July
Early March	Early/Mid May	July

Note These timings are approximate and poorer light conditions in some areas have been taken into account.

SEED SOWING
Sow seeds thinly in seed pans or boxes, lightly covering the seed and firming this to keep the seed coat *below* compost level. Water seed in lightly and cover with paper or a sheet of glass and paper.

PROPAGATION TEMPERATURE
Greenhouse temperatures are particularly important during germination, 65°F. being ideal, 70°F. giving rise to a number of rogue seedlings which result in non-productive plants (see below).

PRICKING OFF
As soon as seedlings can be handled, some three to four days after germination, move into pots of about $4\frac{1}{4}$ in., made either of clay, plastic, bituminised paper or peat. Soil blocks (large size) may also be used. The use of larger pots is favoured these days, as plants can then flower before planting. Plastic pots are gaining popularity as they absorb more heat and require less watering than clay pots, but peat pots on a layer of peat or a solid bench, or contained in boxes with a layer of peat, are easily handled and require less watering.

Use John Innes No. 1 compost, the appropriate U/C mix, or peat compost in all cases. When plants are to be grafted, do not prick off into pots but into boxes, 24 per seed tray. Keep all young seedling plants at around 63–65°F. during the day and 56–58°F. at night, lowering this two or three degrees during dull weather *in the daytime*. High day temperatures increase rate of growth, but reduce the number of flowers on bottom trusses and hasten ripening, exactly the reverse being the case with lower temperatures, i.e. more flowers and therefore bigger bottom trusses, but later ripening. Keep plants well watered, give them plenty of light and space, and if deemed necessary apply a little liquid feeding, preferably with high potash, it being advisable never to let plants go short of nutrients. The correct stage of planting is now considered to be when the first truss has at least one flower open, it having been found that better setting results from this procedure, the plant being 'held' on restraining growth by the swelling of fruit instead of possibly rushing into nonproductive growth.

PREPARATIONS FOR PLANTING
Border culture, including grafted plants
Borders should be well turned over to a good depth during winter and where fresh soil (unsterilised) is being used, some well rotted farmyard manure dug in at 1 cwt. per 10 to 12 sq. yds. can be used. Alternatively peat or clean leaf mould can be used instead of F.Y.M. It is always advisable to have border soil analysed, whether fresh or otherwise, asking specifically for an eelworm count. If there is any doubt about soil, sterilise chemically or by heat (see page 73).

Apply lime by scattering on, flooding in lightly with a fine mist, during January or sufficiently long before planting to bring the pH level of the soil to 6.5, using this in quantities according to the soil analysis recommendations. Ground limestone is preferable to hydrated lime, but this is not essential. This watering, if prolonged enough, will also serve to flush excess salts from the soil, although this also is a matter to be confirmed by soil analysis.

Tomato base fertiliser is applied at 6 to 8 oz. per sq. yd. 10 to 12 days before planting (although it can be used immediately before planting if necessary), raking soil down to a fine tilth in preparation for planting. Apply *standard* tomato base fertiliser for fresh or chemically sterilised soil, *high potash* tomato base fertiliser where soil has been heat sterilised. If in a very mild area, the latter should also be used for chemically sterilised soil, especially when metham sodium sterilants have been used.

The following is the formula for those wishing to make up their own base dressings:

The John Innes Base: 2 parts hoof and horn meal
2 parts superphosphates of lime
1 part sulphate of potash

which contains approximately 6% nitrogen, 7% phosphoric acid and 10% potash, and can therefore be considered as in between standard and high potash base. Adding an extra part of hoof and horn meal is perhaps desirable for older unsterilised soils.

PLANTING

Plant only when soil temperature has reached 56–57° F., confirming this by the use of a good soil thermometer which will depict warmth of soil as opposed to air temperature. More trouble is caused by planting tomatoes in cold soil than many gardeners realise, the roots of the plant being subjected to a check which results in the easy entry of weak parasitic diseases, and these will manifest themselves gradually as the season progresses.

PLANTING OUT DISTANCES AND PLANT ARRANGEMENT

These vary according to the orientation of the house. Where the ridge of the house runs north/south it matters little how the plants are arranged, but where the ridge runs east/west planting too closely, especially along the south facing side, will shade the rest of the plants. In general allow 20 to 24 in. apart, or perhaps a little less than this for later crops and a little more for grafted plants which tend to be vigorous.

Plant firmly and not too deeply in damp (not dry) soil, digging the hole in the correct place with a trowel. After planting water in lightly, using sufficient water only to wet the ball. The decision to remove or leave the variety root with grafted plants can largely depend on the suspected presence of Verticillium wilt from previous crop history, as this disease can travel up the non-resistant variety root into the plant. Generally speaking both roots are planted to avoid the serious check to growth which can result from the severe root

Good shape and firmness are
essential features in tomato growing

A well-hearted greenhouse lettuce early
in the season never fails to please

disturbance associated with the variety root removal.

As distinct from soil temperature, greenhouse air temperature must be of a reasonable order, preferably around 65°F. day and 58°F. night. Obviously temperatures will tend to vary a little, as few amateurs are able to be as precise as commercial growers with their sophisticated control equipment, but low day temperatures will have a very adverse effect on fruit setting. Vent or fan operating thermostats should be set to open ventilators when the temperature rises to around 70–74°F.

WATERING, FEEDING AND TRAINING

The moisture needs of tomatoes vary a great deal according to weather. For the first few weeks, only plants which wilt should be given ball watering, the object being to develop a good root system. A good daily spray with a fine rose, especially during dry sunny weather, will help to keep the atmosphere moist and encourage rooting, along with good vigorous growth and the setting of trusses, provided temperatures are around 65°F. The following table gives water requirements for plants *over* 3 ft. tall and *arbitrary* adjustment will be required for young plants. It is highly important *not* to overwater young plants, as this can check them badly.

Weather	Water needed per plant per day (Full 24 hours)
Very dull (cloudy and dull all day)	$\frac{1}{4}$–$\frac{1}{2}$ pint per plant
Dull (overcast most of the time)	$\frac{1}{2}$–$\frac{3}{4}$ pint per plant
Fairly sunny (cloudy, bright periods)	$1\frac{1}{4}$–$1\frac{1}{2}$ pints per plant
Sunny (only occasional cloud)	2–$2\frac{1}{4}$ pints per plant
Very sunny (clear sky all day)	3–$3\frac{1}{4}$ pints per plant

It should be noted that this ranges from $3\frac{1}{2}$ pints to almost 3 gal. per week, so very careful calculation and observation is required to make good use of these figures. About 2 gal. per week per plant is a fair average.

FEEDING

The feeding of tomatoes can be achieved in a variety of ways. Some gardeners feed with a 1 : 200 or 1 : 300 dilution of liquid feed at every watering, a simple operation if a dilutor is available. Others feed only every 7 to 10 days with liquid feed, largely based on the appearance of the plant, the same applying to the application of dry fertilisers which can be lightly watered in. Modern views centre round controlling growth by keeping the solution of fertilisers in the soil at the right concentration, this being called 'osmotic' feeding, and this is undoubtedly associated with controlled liquid feeding. A still further school of thought is that when both farmyard manure and base fertiliser have been applied, the plants should not be fed at all until well into the season. The best compromise, I feel, is to wait until the first truss of fruit is fully set and the young fruits are the size of a marble before embarking on the chosen feeding method unless it is thought that the plants look starved.

OBSERVATION OF GROWTH

The real secret of success with tomato nutrition is observation of growth. Hard stunted plants are short of nitrogen, lush leggy plants are short of potash, and it is simple to vary the feed according to the symptoms, applying balanced feeds when growth appears balanced.

FEEDING PROGRAMME FOR TOMATOES

Tomato plants normally require more potash early in the season, especially in steam sterilised soil, rather less potash being necessary in chemically sterilised or unsterilised soil. As the season goes on and the plants start to use up the reserves of nitrogen in the soil, the amount of nitrogen given can be increased, until at the end of the season still more nitrogen is given. This pattern of feeding can be achieved by the use of high potash, standard and high nitrogen feeds of the following percentages, this being the formulae widely used in commercial circles.

| K_2O to N RATIO | COMPOSITION (OZ/GALL) | | | NUTRIENTS (LB/10GL) | |
	Potassium Nitrate	Urea or	Ammonium Nitrate	K_2O	N
3:1 (High Potash)	24	—	—	6.3	2.0
2:1 (Standard)	25	5	6	6.3	3.3
1:1 (High Nitrogen)	24	16	20	6.3	6.3

The solution prepared to the above formula is called 'stock' solution, and smaller quantities can of course be made up by scaling the ingredients down proportionately. The best plan, however, is to make up a quantity of stock solution and store this in a tight bottle. Dissolving the ingredients is much easier in *hot* water. Note that these feeds should be applied at a constant dilution of 1:200, which means 1 fl. oz. of the stock solution to $1\frac{1}{4}$ gal. of water, to be applied every 10–14 days after the first truss of fruit is set, or continuously if desired.

Alternatively, proprietary solid and liquid feeds can of course be bought, and these should be used strictly according to directions, the dilution rate generally being higher. For dry feeding sulphate of ammonia, dried blood or urea formaldehyde (nitroform) can be used as a source of nitrogen at rates of around 1 oz. per sq. yd., and sulphate of potash, as possibly the only source of potash, is used at up to $\frac{1}{2}$ oz. per sq. yd. These dry nutrients should also be applied every 10–14 days after the first truss of fruit is set, being flushed in with water, taking care not to damage the neck of the plant. Feeding should again be according to observation of growth.

SUPPORT AND TRAINING
Plants should be supported almost immediately after planting with either tomato fillis or plastic string by winding a loose loop with a non-slip knot around the stem slightly above ground level, the string being attached to strong wires at a height of 6 ft. 6 in., or 7 ft., if this is possible. Alternatively tall canes can be used and the plants tied to these, but this method is less satisfactory. Side shoots are removed regularly, preferably early in the morning, or in the evening when turgid, the plants, as they climb, being regularly twisted around the string or tied to the canes. As the season progresses, bottom leaves are removed by careful snapping off, to allow free circulation of air, but *only* when they show signs of disease or yellowing and *not* when green and healthy.

MULCHING
The application of a top dressing of peat or *well rotted* farmyard manure is a useful technique, both for moisture conser-

vation and the encouragement of surface roots. It can be conveniently carried out when the lower leaves of the plant have been removed.

SEASONAL TREATMENT

Regular watering (see page 129), feeding, adequate temperatures of 65° F. day and 58–60° F., and adequate ventilation at 70–74° F. is the 'blueprint' to aim at with tomatoes. Any irregularities such as non-feeding, and particularly large day-night temperature variations, will frequently give rise to unbalanced growth, and also faulty setting (non-formation of fruit). Gross unproductive growth will certainly occur where low night/high day temperatures prevail, and excess carbohydrates remain in the leaves, causing them to curl and discolour. Disease too can rapidly develop where environmental conditions are unfavourable. Certain maladies such as fruit splitting during irregular weather are inevitable, as indeed are spells of faulty setting, when the fruit may fail to set under the varying temperatures in many amateur greenhouses. A healthy pest and disease free start with the absence of checks is perhaps the most important facet of tomato culture.

The top of the plants should be pinched out when height is restricted or when the season is so advanced that there is little hope of further fruit setting and ripening, this generally being towards the end of August or early September.

RING CULTURE

While ring culture follows a similar pattern to border culture, some cultural modifications are necessary. Planting distances are the same at around 20–24 in. apart. John Innes No. 2 Potting Compost is perhaps the best growing medium, approximately 15 lbs. being required per standard sized container. John Innes No. 3 is often advised, but soil chemists have frequently found that the salt content of this is too high, giving rise to nutritional problems. The soil in the ring dries out rapidly early in the season, as it is freely exposed to the air and this speeds up evaporation. Constant vigilance against dryness is therefore essential, and any surplus water will of course drain quickly into the aggregate. As the plant roots start to grow into the aggregate, the rings will not dry out so badly. Once a vigorous root system has developed in the aggregate, this should be kept moist in addition to the regular watering of the rings. Eventually the total watering requirements will not be very different from border grown plants, much of the water requirement being given through the aggregate. Feeding, training and everything else follows a similar pattern to border culture, although it will be found that early growth is, on the whole, more restricted, and therefore more productive of fruit.

GROWING IN LIMITED QUANTITIES OF SOIL
More or less the same ring culture pattern follows here, it being important to have adequate water at the outset.

STRAW BALE CULTURE
The exact procedure for straw bale culture is often thought to be complicated, when in effect it is fairly simple. The bales, or parts of them, are placed conveniently in a row or rows around the outside and in the centre of the house. Some three weeks before planting the glasshouse air temperature is raised to 50°F. and the bales are thoroughly *soaked* with water on repeated occasions over several days.

Thereafter $\frac{3}{4}$ lb. nitro-chalk should be lightly watered in to each of the bales of approximately 50 lbs. size (proportionately less for sections of bales), followed by a further $\frac{1}{2}$ lb. a few days later. Later still, $1\frac{1}{2}$ lbs. nitro-chalk, 9 oz. potassium nitrate and 6 oz. magnesium sulphate are watered in. The bales should now heat rapidly to 110–130°F. in the centre, and frequent watering will be necessary to keep the bales wet. Once the temperature falls to around 100°F. in the centre of the bale, a 6 in. ridge of John Innes Potting Compost No. 2 or U/C Summer Mix is run along the middle of the bales and allowed 24 hours or so to warm up. The plants are then set out about 12–14 in. apart, usually about three per bale, although if the bales are set closely together it matters little if a plant is at the edge of the bale.

Plants must be watered in and thereafter, by careful inspection, water should be regularly applied as the heat generated by the bales causes rapid drying out. Support can be achieved either by tying the plants to overhead wires with string, or by long wires pushed into the bales, the latter method being preferable as the bales will sink during the season as they decompose. Training out the plants in V formation where space allows gives the closely set plants more room. High potash feeding is usually necessary later in the season to ensure high fruit quality, due to the ready supply of nitrogen from the decomposing bales. Normal side shoot removal and training should be carried out and results will generally be excellent, few, if any, of the plants suffering from root disorders because of the high temperature level of the growing medium. The main problem is watering. Maintaining an adequate supply of water can be time consuming, although some gardeners find that drapes of polythene help in this direction once the season is well advanced, and certainly during holiday periods. A trickle system of watering has much to commend it for straw bales.

END OF SEASON
It is important at the end of the season that plants are removed with as much root as possible, and the haulms disposed of as far away from the greenhouse as possible or burned. Opportunity should be taken at this time to thoroughly clean down the inside of the greenhouse to avoid carrying over troubles.

VARIETIES
There are a great many varieties available today, and all have varying characteristics of growth, quality, shape of fruit, and in some cases resistance to disease, especially leaf mould disease (cladosporium) and now tomato mosaic virus (TMV). Many modern varieties are F.1 hybrids – the seed must be produced annually under controlled conditions.

The following symbols refer to vigour group, which includes the general nature of growth, but modern plant breeders can quickly change the habit of growth.

T/S = Tall spreading.
I   = Intermediate.
C   = Compact
Those marked with * are resistant to various strains of leafmould (Cladosporium) disease. (A.B. or both).

F. I. Hybrids

'Ailresist'*	'Ailsa Craig' type – good for poor light areas (T/S)
'Amberley Cross'*†	Early, heavy cropper, greenback-free (T/S)
'Asix Cross'*	Heavy and early cropper (C)
'Bonset'*	Early variety. Verticillium resistant (I)
'Eurocross' A*	Non-greenback fruit. Excellent colour and quality (I)
'Eurocross' B*	Large round fruits. Excellent for early forcing on heavy soils (I)
'Eurocross' BB*	Large multi-locular fruit. Very early heavy cropper (I)
'Florissant'*	Vigorous. Yield and quality excellent (T/S)
'Globoset'*	'Ailsa Craig' type for heated or cold greenhouses (T/S)
'Growers Pride'*	Early and vigorous (T/S)
'Harrisons' Syston Cross'*	Short-jointed, free setting type. Fruit of good quality and colour. Good for cool greenhouses (C)
'Ijsselcross'*	Non-greenback. Vigorous with larger fruit than Maascross. 'Moneymaker' type (T/S)
'Kingley Cross'*†	Non-greenback. Short jointed, high yielding (C)
'M.G.'*	Ailsa Craig Type (T/S)
'M.M.'*	'Moneymaker' Type (T/S)
'Moneyglobe'*	Excellent quality & high yield. Free setter and earlier than 'Moneymaker' (I)
'Plusresist'*	Early semi-greenback. Suitable for heated or cold greenhouse (I)
'Rijncross'*	Semi-greenback. Vigorous with well shape fruit (T/S)
'Selsey Cross'*†	Non-greenback. Heavy cropper (T/S)
'Seriva'*	More vigorous & heavy cropper than 'Moneymaker'. Large fruit, non-greenback (T/S)

'Supercross'*	Non-greenback fruit similar to that of 'Moneymaker'. Resistant to Tomato Mosaic Virus (I)
'Virocross'*	Resembles Supercross, but semi-greenback slightly larger fruit. Resistant to Tomato Mosaic Virus (I)

† = Varieties bred by the Glasshouse Crops Research Institute

Straight varieties

'Ailsa Craig'	Fruit medium sized and well shaped. (T/S)
'Craigella'	'Ailsa Craig' type. Non-greenback. (T/S)
'Dutch Victory'	Non-greenback. Grown in Holland for the English market. (I)
'E.S. 1'	Early cropper. 'Ailsa Craig' type. (T/S)
'E.S. 5'	Heavy cropper. Fruit of excellent colour and quality. (T/S)
'Exhibition'	Heavy cropper. Even-fruited.
'Harrisons First in the Field'	Good cropper. Early.
'J.R. 6'*	Short-jointed, free-setting.
'Market King'	Heavy cropper. Indoor or outdoor type. (T/S)
'Melville Castle'	Short-jointed. Fruit round and solid.
'Minibelle'	Selection from original cross 'Baby Lea' X 'E.S. 5'. (C)
'Minimonk'	'Moneymaker' type, but of compact habit. (C)
'Moneycross'	Earlier than 'Moneymaker'. High yield. Well shaped fruit.
'Moneymaker'	Very popular. Non-greenback type of medium size and good cropper. Well shaped fruit of good colour. (I)
'Potentate'	Very heavy, early cropper. (I)
'Potential'	Similar to above. Fruits of better quality. (I)

'The Amateur'	Bush variety. Suitable for cloches. Early.

Yellow varieties

'Golden Sunrise'	Early, medium sized even-shaped fruit on strong trusses.
'Mid-day Sun'	Golden orange, medium sized fruit. Does well outdoors. Vigorous.

24 Other greenhouse crops

CUCUMBERS

Few gardeners devote whole greenhouses to this crop, the desire mainly being to grow a plant for harvesting in the salad season; neither is the culture of really early cucumber popular, and they are therefore frequently grown on a bench when this is free of the various early season propagating activities. Cucumbers are a surprisingly simple crop to grow, offering few complications. Sow the seed from February onwards by pushing one seed sideways into a 3- or 4-in. pot containing John Innes No. 1 or other suitable compost. Peat pots are extremely useful in this instance. With a temperature of 60–65°F. germination should take place in 48 hours, seedlings appearing later being discounted, as they lack vigour. Move into 4–5-in. pots when plants are 6 to 8 in. tall and support with a small stake. The commercial way of growing cucumbers is on a 2 ft. high ridge, the ideal compost being an equal mixture of good loamy soil and well rotted farmyard manure. Alternatively John Innes No. 2 Potting Compost will give excellent results, although this may tend to dry out quickly. Soil and greenhouse air temperature should be around 65°F. before the plants are set out at least 2 ft. apart. The need for detailed training is often over-emphasised, and in practice all that is required is support for the plants by either tying on to horizontal wires, merely keeping them to reasonable limits, or treating them as tomatoes and training up strings, when the foliage must be considerably restricted. Male flowers, which have no little embryo cucumber behind the petals, are removed regularly, as pollinated fruits are undesirable. Give adequate water all season, top dress with soil + F.Y.M. when roots are seen on the surface and, if necessary, during very hot weather shade the glass, in addition to giving adequate ventilation. Frequent sprayings with water will maintain the moist muggy atmosphere which cucumbers love, although this, coupled with shading, can give rise to problems when there are other crops to consider, as is frequently the case.

Cucumbers can also be grown on straw bales, using the same procedure described for tomatoes (see page 125), it being advisable, however, to use soil + F.Y.M. instead of compost for the ridge and also to top dress regularly with soil + F.Y.M. They can also be grown in boxes of soil/manure, or even very large pots.

Varieties

'Best Seller'	Early, long dark green fruits. Prolific.
'Bitspot'	Strong growing, heavy, short handled fruit. Dark green, resistant to disease.
'Feminex'	100% female flowers. Very productive. Excellent fruits. Resistant to Scab and leaf-spot.
'Green Spot' –	Ribbed and spined. Excellent for cold and heated houses.
'Market Cross'	Vigorous, disease-resistant. Hothouse cucumber. Fruits particularly handsome.
'Spottex'	Early, hardy and very prolific.
'Top Score'	Dark green medium long fruits. Almost no male flowers. Heavy cropper. Resistant to gummosis
'Simex'	and spot disease.

LETTUCE

The culture of lettuce in a greenhouse or frame is becoming increasingly popular, as salads become a more frequent part of our diet irrespective of season. It is important to realise that modern varieties of lettuce have been specially produced for greenhouse culture, particularly during the short, dull days, and in consequence we have the so-called 'short day' varieties. The timing for lettuce growing varies considerably according to region, but the following is the fairly generally accepted pattern for most areas:

SEED SOWING PERIOD	PLANTING IN GREENHOUSE OR FRAME	CUTTING	COMMENTS
Mid September	Mid October	December	These are difficult crops for poor light areas
November	December	Feb.–March	
December	January	Late March/April	
January	February*	April/May	
February	March*	May	
February*	Planting outside in soil blocks during March/April	May/June	

* No heat required.

Seed may be sown in a variety of ways but, most commonly, thinly in boxes of John Innes Seed Compost, U/C mix, or peat compost. The seedlings are planted out when large enough into borders which have been well dug, brought to a pH of 6.5 and dressed with tomato base fertiliser at 6 to 8 oz. per sq. yd. Pricking out into peat 'thumb' pots is also popular, planting then being delayed until the plants have developed to some extent.

It is commercial practice to dust the soil with Dichloran as a pre-planting precaution against botrytis. Planting distance varies from 7 × 7 in. for small varieties or during poor light periods, to 8 × 8 in. for larger varieties, or all varieties during better light conditions.

Lettuce are surprisingly hardy and can stand cold, although this delays growth and may interfere with the development of certain greenhouse varieties, as well as affecting their tenderness. A temperature of 45–50° F. is adequate for winter crops, with ventilation above 65° F., especially during the spring period when excess heat may cause burning of leaf tips and also prevent hearting. It is important to plant in damp soil and keep the plants well watered, preferably with a fine mist rose on a hose pipe, and this should be carried out after the plants develop 2 or 3 leaves, early in the day so that plants do not lie wet overnight. Success with lettuce in a greenhouse lies in a fast but steady period of uninterrupted growth from the time of planting until cutting.

It is common practice to follow lettuce with tomatoes, in which case the ground should be well forked and a dressing of Hoof and Horn Meal applied at 2 to 3 oz. per sq. yd. before planting with tomatoes, otherwise nitrogen starvation may ensue.

Lettuce varieties for growing under glass

(WS = White Seed; BS = Black Seed).

'Amplus re-selected'	Short day variety for winter and spring heading. Large leaved – heat required.
'Cannington Forcing'	Winter variety. Smooth mid-green leaves. Resistant to some strains of lettuce mildew.
'Cheshunt Early Giant'	For greenhouse forcing only. Hearts well during dull conditions.
'Delta'	Medium leaves. Excellent for spring crops in cold greenhouse or frame.
'Kloek'	Tender green lettuce. Grow in cold or slightly heated greenhouse in autumn. Ideal for forcing under glass in spring.

'Kordaat'	Specially bred for heated greenhouse in late winter or can be grown cold for autumn cutting. Fine round heads.
'Kwiek'	Quick grower, larger firm heads. Grow in cold or slightly heated greenhouse in autumn and in slight heat for spring culture.
'May Princess'	Mosaic tested. Attractive colour and good head size for both frame and cold house.
'Neptune'	Mosaic tested. Winter forcing variety for cropping during December/March. Minimum night temperature of 45–50°F.
'Proeftuins Blackpool'	Suitable as a short day lettuce in heated greenhouses.
'Profos'	Medium-large leaved. Fast growing variety for March/April. Short day lettuce.
'Toinika'	Short day variety for February/April cutting.
'Valentine'	Mosaic tested. Winter forcing for cropping during December to March. Minimum night temperature of 45–50°F.
'Vitesse'	Outstanding variety. Very popular commercially – heated or cold – for spring cutting.

Varieties for sowing under glass and planting out of doors

'All the Year Round'	Mosaic-tested. Very hardy. Solid, pale green heart. Crisp and tender.
'Borough Wonder'	Mosaic tested. May be sown during spring/summer/autumn. Solid hearts, rather pale green in colour. Very popular commercially.

'Buttercrunch'	Semi-hearted, semi-gathering type. Central leaves very crisp and excellent for salad. Dark green plants or medium size and distinct from normal cabbage lettuce.
'Favourite'	Summer variety with large crisp heart and pale green crimpled leaves.
'Suzan'	First-class butter-head variety. Slightly paler than 'Imp. Trocadero'. Very good sized head.
'Trocadero Improved'	Mosaic Tested. Summer or winter variety. Minimum of outside leaves. Hearts medium sized and very compact.
'Webb's Wonderful' WS	Mosaic tested. Summer variety. Large solid crisp heart. Leaves well curled.

Note: Some lettuce varieties can be obtained in pelleted form, which means that they can be space sown or sown individually in peat pots.

MELONS

These are a delicious fruit to grow and very simple to handle. As with cucumber it is most likely that only a few plants will be grown, and a bench offers the most convenient situation after general propagation activities have ceased, generally in April or May. Alternatively a section of the border can be used, preferably on the sunny side of the greenhouse.

Seed is sown in March and early April, using one seed per pot, on its side as for cucumbers, and preferably using peat pots to avoid planting checks. These are filled with John Innes No. 1 or other suitable compost. Prepare the beds, mixing a 2 ft. mound of soil with about $\frac{1}{5}$th to $\frac{1}{6}$th part of well rotted manure, followed by a dressing of tomato base fertiliser (medium potash) at about 8 oz. per bushel. Alternatively John Innes No. 2 compost can be used. Set the plants proud of the soil to avoid disease and give plenty of warmth. The plants are stopped by pinching out the growing shoot, the laterals which develop being trained carefully to horizontal wires or a light temporary framework or wood, such as a section of trellis. Some further training is required, but I have found that (like cucumbers) this need not follow the definite pattern often deemed necessary, the plants simply being kept in reasonable limits. Pollination must be carried out by stripping off the male flowers and stroking these over the female flowers, and while a number of flowers may be pollinated, only allow four fruits to develop per plant, supporting these eventually in little string nets which can be specially bought for the purpose, or can easily be made from old netting. The fruit is ready when a sweet aroma pervades the air. Water and feeding needs are constant, especially when fruit is swelling, although both may be reduced when the fruit is large enough.

Varieties

'Best of all'	Green flesh, finely netted.
'Blenheim Orange'	Delicate flavour. Rich scarlet flesh.
'Hero of Lockinge'	Early, white fleshed. Free setting and prolific.

Canteloupe (Frame) varieties (raised in greenhouse for cold frame growing)

'Charentais'	Early medium sized fruit. Delicious flavour. Deep orange flesh.
'Dutch Net or Spot'	Free setting, medium sized fruit.
'Ogen'	Early, small fruited variety.
'Prescotts'	Large-fruited, scarlet flesh, mid-season.
'Tiger'	Early. Flat medium sized fruit, orange flesh.

MUSTARD AND CRESS

This is a useful crop which more gardeners should grow. The seed of mustard (or rape in winter) and cress are merely pressed into the surface of a suitable receptable, and if left dark for a few days either by covering or by placing under a shrouded bench. The seedlings will be ready for cutting in 10–14 days according to the level of heating and the prevailing weather, being harvested with a large pair of scissors.

FRENCH BEANS

These are specially useful for growing in a lean-to type greenhouse where there is sufficient height of south facing wall. The seeds are best sown during March in little peat pots for planting out in a well dug and manured border during April, 18 inches apart. The plants must be supported with string or canes and kept to within reasonable limits by trimming. Give adequate water, warmth, and a light spraying in the morning of a sunny day. Dwarf beans may be grown in much the same way in 8-in. (4–5 seeds) pots, half-filled initially, or in 10-in. (5–6 seeds) pots, using John Innes Potting Compost No. 2. When the plants are approximately 6 in. high further compost is added.

Varieties

Climbing:	'Tender & True'
	'Early Blue Lake Stringless'
Dwarf:	'Blue Bush Lake'
	'The Prince'

STRAWBERRIES

The practice of forcing strawberries has become widespread commercial practice, especially in Belgium and Holland. Gardeners can also conveniently grow a few plants in pots, selecting healthy young runners for rooting into 3-in. pots, sunk in the ground, during June and July. Pot the plants when large enough into 6-in. pots with John Innes No. 2 Potting Compost and place these on polythene in a vacant cold frame, giving protection only during very severe weather, the object being to induce a semi-dormant plant. The plants are brought into the greenhouse in December or January and given a little water and mild heat until flowering, when a temperature of 55–60°F. is desirable, although this stage may not be reached for some time. While most strawberries are self-fertile, dusting of the flowers with some cotton wool tied on to a stick will ensure better pollination. Although plenty of water is required, try to keep the fruit

The sweet fresh succulence of
garden strawberries can be enjoyed
months earlier if grown in pots
in a heated greenhouse

Grapes growing in a greenhouse; the hardy 'Black Hamburg' is always a favourite

Cantaloup is the small round ribbed variety of musk-melon

dry and support this as it swells with pieces of wire or other convenient means. According to the temperature and variety, fruit can be ready in April or May.

Varieties

'Royal Sovereign'
'Cambridge Favourite'
'Templar'
'Gorella' (especially good for forcing)

VINES

The aspirations of many gardeners to grow grapes in their greenhouse is frequently thwarted by lack of room. While vine rods can be relatively well behaved when young, they are vigorous growers and may eventually make large demands on space, which creates problems when other plants are grown in the same greenhouse. Ideally vines are planted in special borders of rotted turves laced with liberal quantities of bone meal and sulphate of potash, but this procedure is seldom possible in the average greenhouse, especially as the roots will eventually take up a considerable area.

Alternatively, and more preferably, the vines can be planted in a well prepared border outside the greenhouse, the stem being led into the greenhouse just above ground level. This system, apart from giving the root a free run, is less demanding as far as water supplies are concerned.

2–3 year old rods are obtained, and if more than one is grown, plant at least 3 ft. apart. Early crops of grapes can be produced by the application of heat at first at the 45°F. level, followed by gradual raising to 65–70°F. during flowering, a level temperature of 65°F. being maintained thereafter. Many gardeners do not have this specialist approach, however, and vines take pot luck along with the other plants. Correspondingly growth and fruit formation will be delayed or reduced in quantity, but this is not generally a vital matter provided sufficient heat is available to ensure that the fruit has sufficient time to ripen. No fruit should be taken from new rods for one or even two years to avoid early strain, the flowers which form merely being removed. Terminal growth is trained in the most convenient area of the house, a single rod being desirable in the small greenhouse. In December the main rod is cut back to about one half or one third of the season's growth, and the laterals are cut back to two or three plump buds, these being readily seen in the area of the lateral junction. When growth starts annually allow two laterals to develop initially, reducing this to one in each direction every 12 in., tying these securely to wires. When it is decided to allow fruiting, let flower trusses form and pinch out the leading shoot two leaves beyond the flower truss. Drastic thinning of the grapes should be carried out after they start to swell, generally to 1 in. apart, with a pair of vine-thinning scissors.

It is important to maintain adequate watering, and at regular intervals use balanced liquid feeding, especially when fruits are swelling.

Vine growing is frequently made to appear very complicated, but I feel that success in the small greenhouse lies in ruthless annual pruning in January, or better still December, followed also by drastic curtailment during the growing season, as vines have remarkable recuperative powers and seldom resent such hard treatment.

Varieties

'Muscat of Alexander'   (white)
'Black Hamburg'   (black)

PEACHES AND NECTARINES

Lack of space again makes the growing of peaches and nectarines difficult in the amateur sized greenhouse and I think that a tall lean-to structure offers the best scope for their culture. Obtain fan trained 2 to 3 year old trees and plant in a well drained loamy border, tying the branches on to horizontally trained wires. Training simply consists of tying in a proportion of conveniently placed new shoots during the year, removing all badly placed growth, especially that growing outward. A proportion of old wood is then cut out in the autumn. Elaborate pruning procedure need not be followed, much revolving around maintaining a good open shape and keeping growth under control. Flowering will take place according to prevailing temperatures, generally around February/March or even earlier, and pollination is assisted with a rabbit's tail or brush. The little fruits which form gradually are thinned out from time to time to one per square foot. Plenty of moisture at the roots, coupled with daily spraying of the leaves in the morning, is essential for the culture of these plants.

Varieties

Peaches:	'Hales Early'
	'Peregrine' (for the cooler house)
	'Royal George'
Nectarines:	'John Rivers'
	'Amsden June'

FORCED VEGETABLES
An early bite always seems so much tastier and can easily be achieved with a little planning. Main crops are Seakale, Mint, Rhubarb and Asparagus.

Seakale: Parent plants are lifted in the autumn and, after side shoots are removed and saved for spring planting, the main plants are covered to a depth of 3 in. with good organic soil or old rotted manure in boxes or pots. If given water, heat and darkness, succulent tender shoots will form in a few weeks.

Mint: Lift a few roots in autumn, pack them in boxes or pots with a covering of soil, give plenty of moisture, heat and light, and shoots will soon form.

Rhubarb: This is perhaps the easiest of all vegetables to force. Lift well developed crowns in November, allow them to become thoroughly frosted, then, after trimming the root ball, pack closely together with peat, in complete darkness under a bench, and water heavily. Blanched shoots will form at a rate according to the level of heat available.

Asparagus: Well developed plants are lifted and packed together under a 3-in. layer of damp peat. These should be placed under the greenhouse staging, given plenty of moisture and darkness, and shoots will form quickly.

25 GREENHOUSE TROUBLES

As plants grow more quickly in the congenial atmosphere of a greenhouse, so also do pests and diseases of all forms develop more rapidly. It is unfortunately the case that the artificial environment of a greenhouse predisposes many plants to attacks of pests and diseases, especially where the greenhouse, and the plants it contains, are expected to look after themselves all day. No better case can be made out for environmental control equipment than by citing the catalogue of troubles which can ensue as a result of bad enviornmental conditions. It would be foolish to pretend, however, that by installing automatic ventilation, heating and watering equipment, one can guarantee the complete avoidance of trouble, since there are many variable issues which must also be taken into account. A pest or disease spore can float just as easily into a well-managed greenhouse as into a neglected one, and once in residence can set about its nefarious business. Nor would it be right to convey the impression that in this modern day and age pest and disease controlling chemicals have reached the advanced stage of sophistication which allows any malady to be quickly and effectively dealt with. One further fallacy should, I feel, also be exploded, and this relates to so-called 'routine' pest and disease controlling spraying programmes. Pests and diseases alike have shown all too forcibly in recent years that they can quickly build up a resistance to chemicals, so that instead of a routine programme being successful, it is more likely to be the opposite, and a varied control pattern will therefore achieve better results. It is very clear, however, that a sensible approach to cultural practice will avoid many troubles. Checks to growth upset the physiology of a plant in much the same way as a chill will affect ourselves. Dosing plants to excess with quick acting nutrients, letting them go short of water, allowing a heating system to cut off by mistake at night chilling the plants, forgetting to open ventilators and roasting the plant for a few hours, these are but a few of the things which frequently happen. Yet as an Advisory Officer I still find it difficult to make gardeners appreciate that it is these gross irregularities which spell disaster to their crops, and are often the primary cause of many troubles, the pests and diseases merely coming in as secondary problems to bad culture.

Hygiene too is highly important, and while this is emphasised in any gardening book one cares to look at, I wonder how many gardeners pay much attention to the warning. Many pests and diseases are so small that they cannot be seen by the naked eye, especially in their resting stage. A greenhouse may *look* clean, but in actual fact it can be a convenient resting place for millions of spores or overwintering pests. The only way to make sure that it is not is to flush them out of their comfortable winter homes with stringent washing down with disinfectant or detergent, and as far as soil, pots, boxes etc. are concerned, these must be effectively sterilised, it being as well to realise that soil (or containers) which is sterilised is *not* immunised. In fact soil, when sterilised, is much more vulnerable to pests and diseases, many of which, especially disease spores, abound in their millions in the atmosphere.

Obviously, therefore, there are so many variable issues to be considered that it is impossible to embark on a greenhouse gardening programme without running the gauntlet of troubles – physiological, fungal and insecticidal.

VERY IMPORTANT NOTE
The chemicals referred to in the following notes are listed either in the Agricultural Chemicals Approval Scheme booklet *Chemicals for the Gardener* or in *Approved Products for Growers and Farmers*. It cannot be stressed too strongly that directions given with the product *must* be followed to the letter, and some chemicals listed in the notes may not in fact be available for amateurs. New chemicals for pest and disease control are coming forward all the time.

CROP, PLANT OR GREENHOUSE	DISORDERS	SYMPTOMS	PREVENTION AND CONTROL
General propagation, seed sowing, rooting cuttings, culture of young plants, beddings plants, etc.	Damping off; Pythium Spp; Rhizocotonia Spp; Pytophthora Spp	Base of seedlings and young plants turns light brown and stem constricts. Plant eventually collapses. Cuttings attacked in area of cut part or at compost level. Disease spreads upwards causing collapse	High humidity encourages trouble, also ammonia gas given off by newly heat sterilised soil-containing composts. Pots and boxes should be clean or sterilised with formaldehyde. For antirrhinums and lobelias use soil-less compost. Cheshunt compound can be used before sowing and also for newly germinated seedlings. Zineb or quintozene (PCNB) can also be used, as instructed on product
General propagation, seed sowing, rooting cuttings, culture of young plants, bedding plants, etc.	Grey mould	Attacks cuttings or young plants. Starts as light brown lesion, eventually becoming covered with grey dust-like spores	Again encouraged by high humidity. Especially troublesome in a greenhouse which is allowed to chill overnight. Use Thiram dust as directed on product
Bulbs and corms; Carnations, chrysanthemums, cucumbers, pot plants, tomatoes, lettuce, peaches, nectarines, and crops in general	Aphids of various species. Small flies can be seen on leaves, usually in clusters	Attack leaves, feeding on plant sap, causing distortion and loss of vigour. Virus diseases can also be transmitted by various species.	Use insecticidal spray or atomising fluid or smoke at first sign of attack, changing the nature of the chemical frequently, if possible, to avoid build up of resistance. Malathion, nicotine, derris, BHC, DDT/BHC, are the main chemicals used
Bulbs and corms; chrysanthemeums, tomatoes, and several other crops	Caterpillars; Angle shade moth; Tomato moth	Caterpillars feeding on leaves and flowers, often at night	DDT/BHC smokes and sprays
Bulbs and corms; chrysanthemums	Stem eelworm (Ditylenchus dipsaci) attacks bulbs and other plants. Chrysanthemums attacked by specific eelworm (Apelenchoides ritzems-bosi)	Attack leaves and flowers causing distortion. In chrysanthemums brown blotches are formed on leaves, changing from yellow to bronze and purple	Destroy stock of bulbs and use only fresh soil in future. Chrysanthemums stools can be hot water treated — 115 F. for 5 minutes, or sprayed with parathion on several occasions. This is not advised for amateur gardeners
Narcissus (Daffodils)	Narcissus flies	Eggs laid in or near bulbs in Spring. Produce larvae which tunnel into bulbs,	Bulb suppliers generally ensure that all bulbs are free from infestation by hot water treatment or chemical

			Spray with Dithane at first sign of attack and repeat several times
Narcissus (Daffodils)	Leaf scorch (Stagonospora curtisii)	Leaf tips turn reddish brown, followed by death	
Bulbs and corms; Carnations, chrysanthemums, cucumbers, pot plants generally, tomatoes, inside shrubs	Thrips of various species, small brown or yellowish insects	Attack plants in various ways – sucking sap from leaves or flowers, causing acute distortion of growth. Silvery spots often show, especially on carnations. Breeding is more or less continuous	DDT/BHC smoke varied with Derris, Malathion and Nicotine, applied repeatedly until control is gained. Do Not use DDT for curcurbits
Carnations, chrysanthemums, lettuce, tomatoes	Wireworms (small $\frac{1}{2}-\frac{3}{4}$ in. long yellowish bodied insects)	Eggs laid in May/July. Larvae hatch in a few weeks and eat roots of plants. Persist for 4–5 years	Apply BHC (Gamma) as soil dust
Carnations, tomatoes	Fusarium Wilt (Fusarium oxysporum and F. dianthi and other species)	Carnations and tomatoes are affected in warm areas. Plants wilt badly	Use clean stock and sterilised soil. Use Dithane when disease first appears
All crops	Grey mould (Botrytis cinerea)	Attacks a wide range of plants, causing discolouration of leaves, followed by grey dust-like mould. Spreads extremely rapidly. Tomatoes badly attacked on stems, leaves or fruit. Ghost spot on fruit is caused by partial development of botrytis. Lettuce can also be badly attacked	Keep atmosphere dry by skillful ventilation and application of heat. Avoid severe night temperature drops. Thiram dust or TCNB smoke should be used with care according to directions. Hand paint lesions with creosote on tomato stems
Carnations	Carnation fly	Eggs laid on upper surface of leaves, resulting in larvae which moves into the stem	DDT/BHC smokes
Tulips	'Fire' (Botrytis tulipae)	Deformed shoots, followed by grey spots which eventually run together, resulting in reddish discolouration of leaves	Dithane, Thiram or Quintozene (PCNB) sprays or dust used at first sign of attack and persisted with
Many crops and plants	Earwigs	Bite holes in flowers and stems during night, causing acute distortion and malformation	Trap with inverted pots, and spray or dust with DDT/BHC (not DDT for curcurbits)

Crops/Plants	Pest	Symptoms	Control
Many crops and plants	Red Spider Mite (Tetranychus urticae and T. cinnebarinus)	Nymphs and adults suck sap from leaves, causing yellowing and eventual destruction of leaves. Webs develop on underside of leaves, hindering control	Extremely persistent pests, over-wintering in cracks in cracks in greenhouse. A variety of materials should be used as smokes or sprays to avoid building up resistance. These include azo-benzene, derris, petroleum oil, Malathion and others
Carnations, chrysanthemums, pot plants and shrubs	Powdery mildew (Oidium sp.)	Dirty white powder on leaves, stems and flowers	Karathane spray or dust at first sign of attack
Carnations, chrysanthemums, and other plants	Rust (Uromyces dianthi)	Small blotches on leaves, later releasing reddish brown spores	Thiram, Dithane, Zineb sprays or dusts, at first sign of disease. Overwinters in stools of chrysanthemums
Carnations	Stem rot (Fusarium culmorum) Verticillium wilt (Verticillium cinerescens)	Soil borne disease enters roots and spreads up plant, affecting moisture conducting tissue. Wilt follows,	Adequate soil sterilisation by heat or effective chemicals. Raising greenhouse temperature to 75°F. for a week, combined with surface mulching, can offset trouble. Watering with dithane is reasonably effective
Tomatoes	Verticillium wilt (Verticillium alboatrum)	sometimes only on one side of plant on carnations	
Chrysanthemums	Gall midge (Diarthronomyia chrysanthemi)	Cone-shaped galls form on leaves and stems	Spray with BHC at first sign of attack
Chrysanthemums, lettuce	Stool miner (Paila nigricornis)	Larvae feed on stem base and destroy cutting material	Spray with BHC Spring and Summer to destroy eggs. Lift and destroy all affected stools. With lettuce use BHC before planting after an attack, on a previous crop
Chrysanthemums, pot plants, tomatoes	Leaf miner (Phytomyza and Liriomyza solani)	Eggs laid on leaves produce larvae which tunnel into leaves	BHC aerosol, DDT/BHC smoke, when attack first noticed
Chrysanthemums	Tarnished plant bug or capsid (Lygus rugulipennis)	Bugs suck sap, exuding toxin which twists and distorts. A wide range of plants are attacked out of doors	DDT or Malathion sprays, DDT/BHC smokes
Chrysanthemums, cucumbers, melons, pot plants, tomatoes	White fly (Trialeurodes vaporariorum)	Eggs laid on leaves, hatching into nymphs which suck sap and exude honeydew on which moulds develop. Growth is distorted. In pelargoniums leaf spot may be spread by this pest	A variety of sprays, dusts, aerosols, or smokes can be used, based on, DDT, DDT/BHC (not DDT for curcurbits). All must be used within 14 days and at short intervals to ensure control. Thorough cleaning or fumigating of greenhouse in winter when empty is essential

Crop	Pest/Disease	Description	Control
Chrysanthemums	Petal damping, botrytis, grey mould	'Pin-pointing' of flower, followed by complete flower rot	Improve environment by application of heat, especially at night. TCNB smoke can be used at first sign of attack
Chrysanthemums	Petal blight (tersonilia spp.)	Affects outside petals as water spots and spreads into flower centre	Dithane spray or dust before bud bursting
Chrysanthemums	Ray blight (Mycosphaerella ligulicola)	Mainly attacks inside when growing chrysanthemums on year round culture	Obtain clean stock. Spray with dithane. Difficult to control once in existence
Cucumber	French fly (Tyrophagus sp.)	Introduced on straw (bales or loose). Mites feed on growing plant and leaves, causing pale spots which later develop into holes. Usually disappear in high summer	Nicotine smokes or sprays
Cucumbers, melons, tomatoes	Leaf hoppers (Erythroneura pallidifrons)	Lively insects feeding on leaves cause distortion and restrict growth	Nicotine or malathion at first sign of attack
Cucumber	Fungus gnats of various species	Develop initially on decaying fungi, FYM, or straw bales. Attack roots of plants causing wilting or death	Malathion watered into bed
Cucumbers, melons and other soft plants	Springtails of various species	White six-legged soil pests feeding on soft stems, roots and root hairs in clusters. Some actively jump by means of tails	BHC drenches or dusts
Cucumbers, melons, lettuce, tomatoes and practically all other plants	Symphylid (Scutigerella immaculata)	Very active $\frac{1}{4}$ in. long insects feeding on roots, causing hard or deformed growth. They move down to lower depths of soil in winter or when soil is wet. Worst in highly organic soil	Thoroughly sterilise soil by heat or effective chemicals, such as metham/sodium. Malathion drenches can be reasonably effective
Cucumbers, tomatoes and other plants	Woodlice of various species	Attack plant roots or stems at soil level with drastic effects if in large numbers	Bait with cut turnips, destroy collecting lice with blow lamp. DDT dusts also help
Cucumbers	Black Rot (Mycosphaerella citrullina)	Dieback of laterals at main stem. Identified by small black spots	Dithane spray, coupled with sterilisation of boxes etc. to avoid spread of infection

Host	Trouble	Description	Control
Cucumbers	Gummosis (Cladosporium cucumerinum)	Silver spots on fruit which turn gummy, followed by velvety growth of green fungus	Dithane dust at first sign of attack
Cucumbers	Mildew (Erysiphe cichoracearum)	White felt over leaves	Karathane spray
Lettuce and other crops	Leatherjackets, various species	Tough leathery looking grubs, $\frac{1}{2}$ in.–1 in. long, feed on roots	BHC dusts before planting. Can be very troublesome on new soils
Lettuce	Millipedes, various species	Many-legged 1 in. long creatures attacking roots and stems	Normally feed on organic matter. Adequate soil sterilisation of BHC is most effective
Lettuce, pot plants	Downy mildew (Bremia lactucae and other species)	Yellow areas on upper surface of leaves with grey fungus on correspondingly lower areas	Dithane dust at first sign of attack
Pot plants, peaches, nectarines, vines	Mealy bug (Pseudococcus spp.)	Little bugs covered with waxy secretion cluster on plants and cause distortion or loss of vigour, followed by leaf loss	Nicotine or malathion sprays and dusts. Methylated spirit applied directly to vine stems or peach branches is also effective
Primulas, auriculas, lettuce	Root aphis (Pemphigus auriculae and other sp.)	Clusters of waxy-like insects present on the roots	BHC or nicotine drench
Vines, cyclamens and other plants	Vine weevil (Otiorrhynchus sulcatus)	Eggs laid in soil hatch in 2–3 weeks and white grubs feed on roots, causing wilting	Add BHC to compost if in doubt, or BHC drench at first sign of attack
Cyclamen	Root and corm rots (Cylindrocarpon radicola and Thielviopsis basicoli)	Soil borne disease which attacks and rots corm and roots of cyclamen	Use sterilised compost. Dithane drench is also effective
Roses under glass	The troubles which affect roses under glass are broadly similar to those affecting them out of doors and control measures are the same		
Tomatoes	Potato root eelworm (Heterodera rostochiensis)	Resting cysts start early in season releasing minute larvae which attack root systems, causing browning of lower leaves and wilting of plant. Their activities allow entry of root rots and other diseases	Very difficult to gain complete control in tomato borders, but effective control can be achieved use of metham/sodium in powdered form. Alternative methods of cultivation allowing isolation from borders, using sterilised media, are advisable in bad cases

Crop	Disease	Symptoms	Control
Tomatoes	Root-knot eelworm (Meloidogyne spp.)	Roots attacked, resulting in a deformed and galled appearance. Will rest in soil for 2 years in absence of host plants	Good control achieved with metham/sodium sterilants, also by heat. Failing this, adopt alternative cultural methods
Tomatoes	Brown or corky root rots (Colletotrichum atramentarium and other fungi)	This is a disease complex causing thickened, cracked and discoloured roots, plants suffer severe debility and sometimes die. Presence of potato eelworm can possibly initiate the trouble	Efficient soil sterilisation is the only cure, failing which alternative methods of culture should be used. Plants can also be watered with dithane during growing season
Tomatoes	Buckeye rot	Soil borne spores splash on to fruit causing disfiguring dark brown rings	Take great care when watering, avoiding splashing. Adequate ventilation will also help. Spray with dithane at first sign of attack
Tomatoes	Didymella stem rot (Didymella lycopersici)	Attacks plants at soil level, causing brown-grey sunken lesions which extend up the stem, eventually girdling it, killing plants. Shiny spores may be seen on detailed examination with a lens	Sterilise house thoroughly in winter and get rid of infected haulms well away from greenhouse. Paint bottom of stem with dithane at first sign of attack, and sterilise soil thoroughly by heat
Tomatoes	Leaf mould (Cladosporium fulvum)	Starts as yellow spots on upper surface, with corresponding grey-brown mould patches on lower surfaces. Appearance of disease coincides with periods of still muggy weather, when humidity is high. Once established it can spread rapidly and affect flowers as well as leaves. Has an overall yield reducing effect	Certain districts are notorious for this disease, especially those where humidity is high. It is always advisable to grow resistant varieties in bad areas. When non-resistant varieties are grown, spray with copper, zineb or dithane in season. TCNB smokes can also be used. Good ventilation night and day, coupled with adequate air movement by means of fans or use of heaters, will do much to offset the trouble
Tomatoes	Potato blight (Phytophthora infestans)	More common in the South or where tomatoes are grown out of doors. Brown sunken areas appear on fruit	The same control measures as described for leaf mould should be practised
Tomatoes	Root and foot rot (Phytophthora spp; Pythium spp. Rhizoctonia solani)	Fungi enter through roots or base of stem, especially when plants are subjected to growing checks or soils are unusually wet or previously badly contaminated	Soil sterilisation for the future is essential. Dithane can be used at 3–4 week intervals. Avoid checks to growth (especially planting in cold soil)

Tomatoes	Sclerotinia disease (Sclerotinia sclerotiorum)	Only base of stems attacked. A white mould develops, followed by black resting bodies. Plants wilt and die	Special attention should be paid to sterilisation for the future

PHYSIOLOGICAL DISORDERS

TOMATOES	Blossom end rot	End of fruit develops a black zone	This is caused by inadequate or irregular watering or too high a salt content
	Cracking or splitting of fruit	Where fruit cracks or splits	Due to widely varying environmental conditions and may largely be influenced by type of weather
	Dry set and blossom drop	Where flowers fall off or fruit fails to set	Due again to irregular growing conditions, especially temperatures below 65°F. and above 80°F., also perhaps to virus infection
	Blotchy ripening	Irregular ripening of fruit	Caused by day temperature being too high and by irregular feeding. Go on to regular liquid feeds and keep potash level high
POT PLANTS	Over-watering	Yellowing and wilting of lower leaves	Always ensure that plants are not over-watered by constant supervision. Sometimes low night temperature has the same effect
MANY PLANTS	Over-feeding	Scorched appearance of foliage and leaf tips	Apply less feeding or in more diluted form
	Gross lanky growth	Lack of light	Make sure that plants obtain maximum light, especially in winter, bearing in mind their likes and dislikes in this direction

TEMPERATURE CONVERSION TABLES

E FACTS AND FIGURES

] seeds are contained in 1 oz. of tomato seed

hel of compost is required per 9 boxes (2–3 in. deep)

of compost contains approximately 36 bushels

of seed box : 14 in. x 9 in. x 2 to 3 in. deep

shel measures 22 in. x 10 in. x 12 in. (or 10 in.)

ES ON QUANTITIES

shel of soil $= 1\frac{1}{4}$ cubic feet

. oz. – 1 pint

lespoon $= \frac{1}{2}$ fl. oz.

ssertspoonfuls $=$ 1 tablespoon

spoonfuls $=$ 1 dessertspoonful

llon of water $=$ 1 lb.

°F	°C	°F	°C
86	30.0	65	18.3
85	29.4	64	17.8
84	28.9	63	17.2
83	28.3	62	16.7
82	27.8	61	16.1
81	27.2	60	15.6
80	26.7	59	15.0
79	26.1	58	14.4
78	25.6	57	13.9
77	25.0	56	13.3
76	24.4	55	12.8
75	23.9	54	12.2
74	23.3	53	11.7
73	22.8	52	11.1
72	22.2	51	10.6
71	21.7	50	10.0
70	21.1	49	9.4
69	20.6	48	8.9
68	20.0	47	8.3
67	19.4	46	7.8
66	18.9	45	7.2

Formulae for conversion :

Centigrade to Fahrenheit $= \left(x°C \times \dfrac{9}{5}\right) + 32$

Fahrenheit to Centigrade $= \left(x°F - 32\right) \times \dfrac{5}{9}$

Index